READING
CAN BE CHILD'S PLAY

ABOUT THE AUTHORS

Although father-daughter writing teams are not unknown, they are rather rare. Among them is that of James H. Humphrey and Joy N. Humphrey, whose knowledge and deftness with their subject make them even more unusual.

James H. Humphrey, Professor Emeritus at the University of Maryland is the author of over 40 books and 200 articles and research reports. A notable researcher in the area of reading and active play, his statements on the subject have been translated into four languages and distributed to 55 countries. In addition, his work has been featured on a Voice of America broadcast and distributed to their 35 language centers.

Joy N. Humphrey is a classroom teacher in the public schools of Livonia, Michigan. She has an advanced degree from Johns Hopkins University in the area of Communitive Disorders (reading disabilities, language and learning disabilities). She has had experience as a teacher of slow-learning reading disabled children. This is the eighth book she has coauthored with her father. In addition, she has published several invited chapters of books as well as numerous articles in professional journals.

READING
CAN BE CHILD'S PLAY
An Aid for Teachers

By

JAMES H. HUMPHREY, Ed.D.
Professor Emeritus
University of Maryland
and
JOY N. HUMPHREY, M.S.
Livonia Public Schools
Livonia, Michigan

CHARLES C THOMAS • PUBLISHER
Springfield • Illinois • U.S.A.

Published and Distributed Throughout the World by

CHARLES C THOMAS • PUBLISHER
2600 South First Street
Springfield, Illinois 62794-9265

© *1990 by* CHARLES C THOMAS • PUBLISHER
ISBN 0-398-05657-9
Library of Congress Catalog Card Number: 89-28411

With THOMAS BOOKS *careful attention is given to all details of manufacturing
and design. It is the Publisher's desire to present books that are satisfactory as to their
physical qualities and artistic possibilities and appropriate for their particular use.*
THOMAS BOOKS *will be true to those laws of quality that assure a good name
and good will.*

Printed in the United States of America
SC-R-3

Library of Congress Cataloging-in-Publication Data

Humphrey, James Harry, 1911–
    Reading can be child's play : an aid for teachers / by James H.
Humphrey and Joy N. Humphrey.
        p.   cm.
    Includes bibliographical references.
    ISBN 0-398-05657-9
    1. Reading (Primary)   2. Play.   I. Humphrey, Joy N.   II. Title.
LB1525.24.H86   1990
372.4 — dc20   89-28411
                                                                   CIP

PREFACE

Almost three centuries ago Francois Fénelon, the famous French educator and ecclesiastic, is reputed to have suggested that he had seen certain children who had learned to read while playing. Although we are not exactly sure what he meant, we are willing to rationalize that his statement might have been the first indication that there is a high degree of compatibility between reading and active play experiences, and a forerunner of some of the thoughts and ideas expounded in this book.

Reading Can Be Child's Play has been prepared for teachers, parents and others who are in a position to help children with their reading pursuits. Its purpose is to assist these adults in their efforts to help children learn to read and to improve upon their ability to read.

The initial chapter presents an overview of child development and learning. Chapter 2 summarizes the meaning of reading and the nature of the reading process. Chapter 3 takes into account the theory of learning about reading through active play. The fourth chapter goes into detail with regard to how active play experiences can improve upon the various qualities that are important to children in their efforts to deal with the reading process. Chapters 5 and 6 are devoted to the use of active play in diagnosing reading readiness and developing reading skills. Chapter 7 explains the theory underlying active play reading content. The final three chapters consider active play reading content in the areas of active games, rhythmic play and stunt play, and over 60 active play stories are presented.

All of the practices in the book have been carefully researched and extensively field tested with large numbers of children and have been found to be successful when applied in the appropriate manner.

Any book is seldom the product of authors alone. It is almost always true that many individuals participate, at least indirectly, in some way before a book is finally "put to bed." This volume is no exception. In this regard, we are grateful to the many fellow teachers, reading specialists and, of course, children themselves who have helped us in some way to improve upon our knowledge about the subject of reading.

James H. Humphrey
Joy N. Humphrey

CONTENTS

READING
CAN BE CHILD'S PLAY

Chapter 1

CHILD DEVELOPMENT AND LEARNING

This book is for teachers, parents and other adults who deal in some way with children. Its purpose is to help them help children learn — specifically to learn about reading.

Simply recognizing a child's mannerisms and his or her likes and dislikes does not necessarily mean that an adult has a full understanding of child development and learning. In fact, even those professional workers who spend their time studying about children are not always in complete agreement with regard to the complex nature of child development. The major purpose of this initial chapter is to present general information on this subject. This means that the discussion will be concerned with the so-called "average" child. It should be remembered that averages tend to be arrived at mathematically and that a child develops at his own individual rate. It is quite likely that a child may be above average in some characteristics and below average in others. It is important that adults realize this; thus, the materials in this chapter should be considered with this idea in mind.

MEANING OF TERMS

To avoid confusion, it seems appropriate for us to convey to the reader the meaning of certain terms used in this chapter. The two major terms that we are concerned with are *development* and *learning*.

Development is concerned with changes in the child's ability to function at an increasingly higher level. For example, a stage in development in the infant is from creeping to crawling. This is later followed by the developmental stage of walking when the child moves to an upright position and begins to propel himself over the surface area by putting one foot in front of the other.

Most definitions of *learning* are characterized by the idea that it involves some sort of change in the individual. This means that when an individual has learned, his behavior is modified in one or more ways. Thus, a good standard for learning would be that after having an experience a person could behave in a way in which he could not have behaved before having had the experience. In this general connection, many learning theorists suggest that it is not possible to *see* learning. However, behavior can be seen, and when a change in behavior has occurred, then it is possible to infer that change and learning have occurred. This concept is depicted in the following diagram.

Learning Can be Inferred by a Change in Behavior

Child Behaves → Child is in a Learning → Child Behaves in a Way
in a Given Way   Situation   That is Different from
                                               Before he Was in the
                                               Learning Situation

The essential difference *between* development and learning is that development deals with general abilities while learning is concerned with specific behaviors.

When it is considered that development of children brings about needs and that these needs must be met satisfactorily, the importance of an understanding of development is readily seen. When an understanding of the various aspects of development is accomplished, teachers and parents are then in a better position to provide improved procedures for meeting the needs of children. This implies that we might well be guided by what could be called a developmental philosophy if we are to meet with any degree of success in our dealings with children.

TOTAL PERSONALITY DEVELOPMENT

Total development is the fundamental purpose of the education of children. All attempts at such education should take into account a combination of *physical, social, emotional,* and *intellectual* aspects of human behavior. Thus, these are the forms of development that we will consider in our discussion here. Of course, there are other forms of development, but they can be subclassified under one of these areas. For example, *motor development,* which can be described as progressive change in motor performance, is considered as a part of the broader aspect of *physical development.* In addition, *moral development,* which is concerned with the capacity of the individual to distinguish between standards of right and wrong, could be considered a dimension of the broad aspect of *social development.* This is to say that moral development involving achievement in the ability to determine right from wrong is influential in the individual's social behavior.

A great deal of clinical and experimental evidence indicates that a human being must be considered as a *whole* and not a collection of parts. For purposes here we would prefer to use the term *total personality* in referring to the child as a unified individual or total being. Perhaps a more common term is *whole child.* However, the term *total personality* is commonly used in the field of psychology, and it has been gaining more use in the field of education. Moreover, when we consider it from a point of view of man existing as a person, it is interesting to note that "existence as a person" is one rather common definition of personality.

The total personality consists of the sum of all the physical, social, emotional, and intellectual aspects of any individual; that is, the major forms of development previously identified. The total personality is *one thing* comprising these various major aspects. All of these components are highly interrelated and interdependent. All are of importance to the balance and health of the personality, because only in terms of the health of each can the personality as a whole maintain a completely healthful state. The condition of any one aspect affects each other aspect to a degree and thus the personality as a whole.

When a nervous child stutters or becomes nauseated, a mental state is *not* necessarily causing a physical symptom. On the contrary, a pressure imposed upon the organism causes a series of reactions that include thought, verbalization, digestive processes, and muscular function. It is not that the mind causes the body to become upset; the total organism is upset by a situation and reflects its upset in several ways, including disturbance in thought, feeling, and bodily processes. The whole individual responds in interaction with the social and physical environment, and as the individual is affected by the environment, he or she, in turn, has an effect upon it.

However, because of long tradition during which physical development *or* intellectual development, rather than physical development *and* intellectual development, has been glorified, we are often still accustomed to dividing the two in our thinking. The result may be that we sometimes pull human beings apart with this kind of thinking.

Traditional attitudes that separate the mind and body tend to lead to unbalanced development of the child with respect to mind and body and/or social adjustment. What is more important is that we fail to use the strengths of one to serve the needs of the other.

The foregoing statements have attempted to point out rather forcefully the idea that the identified components of the total personality comprise the unified individual. That each of these aspects might well be considered separately should also be taken into account. As such, each aspect should warrant a separate discussion. This appears extremely important if one is to understand fully the place of each aspect as an integral part of the total personality. The following discussions of the physical, social, emotional, and intellectual aspects of personality should be viewed in this general frame of reference.

The Physical Aspect of Personality

One point of departure in discussing the physical aspect of personality could be to state that "everybody has a body." Some are short, some are tall, some are lean, and some are fat. Children come in different sizes, but all of them have a certain innate capacity that is influenced by the environment.

It might be said of the child that he *is* his body. It is something he can see. It is his base of operation—or what might be termed the *physical base*. The other components of the total personality—social, emotional, and intellectual—are somewhat vague as far as the child is concerned. Although these are manifested in various ways, children do not always see them as they do the physical aspect. Consequently, it becomes all important that a child be helped early in life to gain control over the physical aspect, or what is known as basic body control. The ability to do this, of course, will vary from one child to another. It will likely depend upon the status of *physical fitness* of the child. The broad area of physical fitness can be broken down into certain components, and it is important that individuals achieve to the best of their natural ability as far as these components are concerned. There is not complete agreement as far as identification of the components of physical fitness are concerned. However, the President's Council on Physical Fitness and Sports considers these components to consist of the following:

1. Muscular strength (the contraction power of the muscles).
2. Muscular endurance (ability of the muscles to perform work).
3. Circulatory-respiratory endurance (moderate contractions of large muscle groups for relatively long periods of time).

4. Muscular power (ability to release maximum muscular force in the shortest time).
5. Agility (speed in changing direction, or body position).
6. Speed (rapidity with which successive movements of the same kind can be performed).
7. Flexibility (range of movement in a joint or a sequence of joints).
8. Balance (ability to maintain position and equilibrium).
9. Coordination (working together of the muscles in the performance of a specific task).

The components of physical fitness and, thus, the physical aspects of personality can be measured by precise instruments, such as measurements of muscular strength. Moreover, we can tell how tall a child is or how heavy he or she is at any stage of his or her development. In addition, medically trained personnel can derive other accurate information with assessments of blood pressure, blood counts, and urinalysis.

The Social Aspect of Personality

Human beings are social beings. They work together for the benefit of society. They have fought together in time of national emergencies to preserve the kind of society they believe in, and they play together. While all this may be true, the social aspect of personality still is quite vague and confusing, particularly as far as children are concerned.

It was a relatively easy matter to identify certain components of physical fitness such as strength and endurance. However, this does not necessarily hold true for components of social fitness. The components of physical fitness are the same for children as for adults. On the other hand, the components of social fitness for children may be different from the components of social fitness for adults. By some adult standards children might be considered as social misfits because certain behavior of children might not be socially acceptable to some adults.

To the dismay of some adults, young children are uninhibited as far as the social aspect of personality is concerned. In this regard we need to be concerned with social maturity as it pertains to the growing and ever-changing child. We need to give consideration to certain characteristics of social maturity and how well they are dealt with at the different stages of child development.

Perhaps adults need to ask themselves such questions as: Am I helping the child to become self-reliant by giving him or her independence at the proper time? Am I helping him or her to be outgoing and interested in others as well as in himself or herself? Am I helping the child to know how to satisfy his or her own needs in a socially desirable way?

The Emotional Aspect of Personality

For many years, emotion has been a difficult concept to define; in addition, there have been many changing ideas and theories as far as the study of emotion is concerned.

Obviously, it is not the purpose of a book of this nature to attempt to go into any great depth on a subject that has been one of the most intricate undertakings of psychology for many years. A few general statements, however, do seem to be in order if we are to understand more clearly this aspect of personality.

Emotion is a response a person makes to a stimulus for which he is not adequately prepared. For example, if a child is confronted with a situation and does not have a satisfactory response, the emotional pattern of fear may result. If one finds himself or herself in a position where desires are frustrated, the emotional pattern of anger may occur. It is interesting to note that *reading* is a school subject area that is loaded with emotion and frustration for many children. In fact, one of the levels of reading recognized by reading specialists is called the "frustration level." In behavioral observation terms this can be described as the level in which children evidence distracting tension, excessive or erratic body movements, nervousness and distractibility. This frustration level is said to be a sign of emotional tension or stress with breakdowns in fluency and a significant increase in reading errors. (One of the important aspects of the active play approach—as we shall see later—is that the child is relieved of this emotional stress in this pleasurable approach to reading.)

Emotions might be classified in two different ways: those that are *pleasant* and those that are *unpleasant.* For example, *joy* could be considered as pleasant emotional experience while *fear* would be an unpleasant one. It is interesting that a good proportion of the literature is devoted to emotions that are unpleasant. It has been found that in psychology books much more space is given to such emotional patterns as fear and anger than to such pleasant emotions as joy and contentment.

Generally speaking, the pleasantness or unpleasantness of an emotion seems to be determined by its strength or intensity, by the nature of the situation arousing it, and by the way an individual perceives or interprets the situation. As far as children are concerned, their emotions tend to be more intense than those of adults. If an adult is not aware of this aspect of child behavior, he or she will not likely understand why a child may react rather violently to a situation that to the adult seems somewhat insignificant. It should also be taken into account that different children will react differently to the same type of situation. For example, something that might anger one child might have a rather passive influence on another. In this regard, it is interesting to observe the effect that winning or losing has on certain children.

The Intellectual Aspect of Personality

The word *intelligence* is derived from the Latin word *intellectus,* which literally means the "power of knowing." Intelligence has been described in many ways. One general description of it is the "capacity to learn or understand."

Individuals possess varying degrees of intelligence, and most people fall within a range of what is called "normal" intelligence. In dealing with this aspect of personality we should perhaps give attention to what might be considered some components of intellectual fitness. However, this is a difficult thing to do. Because of the somewhat vague nature of intelligence, it is practically impossible to identify specific components of it. Thus, we need to view intellectual fitness in a somewhat different manner.

For purposes of this discussion we would like to consider intellectual fitness from two different, but closely related points of view: first, from a standpoint of intellectual *needs* and second, from a standpoint of how certain things *influence* intelligence. It might be said that if a child's intellectual needs are being met then perhaps we could also say that he or she is intellectually fit. From the second point of view, if we know how certain things influence intelligence, then we might understand better how to contribute to intellectual fitness by improving upon these factors.

There appears to be some rather general agreement with regard to the intellectual needs of children. Among others, these needs include: (1) a need for challenging experiences at the child's level of ability, (2) a need for intellectually successful and satisfying experiences, (3) a need for the opportunity to solve problems, and (4) a need for the opportunity to participate in creative experiences instead of always having to conform.

Some of the factors that tend to influence intelligence are (1) health and physical condition, (2) emotional disturbance, and (3) certain social and economic factors.

When adults have a realization of intellectual needs and factors influencing intelligence, perhaps then, and only then, can they deal satisfactorily with children in helping them in their intellectual pursuits.

It was mentioned that an important intellectual need for children is the opportunity to participate in creative experiences. This need is singled out for special mention because the opportunities for creative experiences are perhaps more evident in active play situations than in almost any other single aspect of the child's life.

DEVELOPMENTAL CHARACTERISTICS OF CHILDREN

It is important that adults have a general overview of the behavior of children as they progress in their development. This is the intent of the following discussion.

The range of age levels from six through twelve usually includes children from grades one through six. A child is considered a preschooler if he or she is below age six, unless the school system supports a kindergarten. In this case the child would enter school at approximately age five.

In our culture when the child begins his formal education he leaves home and family for a part of the day to take his place with a group of children of approximately the same age. Not only is he taking an important step in becoming increasingly more independent and self-reliant, but as he learns he moves from being a highly self-centered individual to becoming a more socialized group member.

This stage is characterized by a certain lack of motor coordination, because the small muscles of the hands and fingers are not as well developed as the large muscles of the arms and legs. Thus, as he starts his formal education, the child uses large crayons or pencils as a means of expressing himself. His urge to action is expressed through movement and noise. Children at these age levels thrive on vigorous activity. They develop as they climb, run, jump, or keep time to music. An important physical aspect at this level is that the eyeball is increasing in size and the eye muscles are developing. This is an important factor in the child's readiness to see and read small print.

Even though he has a relatively short attention span, he is extremely curious about his environment. At this stage an adult can capitalize upon the child's urge to learn by providing opportunities for him to gain firsthand experiences through the use of the senses. He sees, hears, smells, feels, tastes, and of course plays in order to learn.

As the child progresses through various stages in his or her development, certain distinguishing characteristics can be identified, which provide implications for adult guidance.

The detailed description of the characteristics given here includes the age levels five through twelve. It should be understood that these characteristics are suggestive of the behavior patterns of the so-called "normal" child. This implies that if a child does not conform to these characteristics, it should not be interpreted to mean that he or she is seriously deviating from the normal. In other words, it should be recognized by an adult that each child progresses at his or her own rate and that there can be much overlapping of the characteristics listed for each age level. A case in point is the range of heights and weights given in the following detailed lists of characteristics. These heights and weights are what might be called "a range within a range" and are computed averages within larger ranges. In other words, children at a given age level could possibly weigh much more or less and be much taller or shorter than the range indicates.

Characteristics of Five-Year-Old Children

Physical Characteristics

1. Boys' height, 42 to 46 inches; weight, 38 to 49 pounds; girls' height, 42 to 46 inches; weight, 36 to 48 pounds.
2. May grow 2 or 3 inches and gain from 3 to 6 pounds during the year.
3. Girls may be about a year ahead of boys in physiological development.
4. Beginning to have better control of body.
5. The large muscles are better developed than the small muscles that control the fingers and hands.
6. Usually determined whether he will be right- or left-handed.
7. Eye-hand coordination is not complete.
8. May have farsighted vision.
9. Vigorous and noisy, but activity appears to have definite direction.
10. Tires easily and needs plenty of rest.

Social Characteristics

1. Interest in neighborhood games that involve any number of children.
2. Plays various games to test his skills.
3. Enjoys other children and likes to be with them.
4. Interests are largely self-centered.
5. Seems to get along best in small groups.
6. Shows an interest in home activities.
7. Imitates when he plays.
8. Gets along well in taking turns.
9. Respects the belongings of other people.

Emotional Characteristics

1. Seldom shows jealousy toward younger siblings.
2. Usually sees only one way to do a thing.
3. Usually sees only one answer to a question.
4. Inclined not to change plans in the middle of an activity but would rather begin over.
5. May fear being deprived of mother.
6. Some definite personality traits evidenced.
7. Is learning to get along better but still may resort to quarreling and fighting.
8. Likes to be trusted with errands.
9. Enjoys performing simple tasks.
10. Wants to please and do what is expected of him.
11. Is beginning to sense right and wrong in terms of specific situations.

Intellectual Characteristics

1. Enjoys copying designs, letters, and numbers.
2. Interested in completing tasks.
3. May tend to monopolize table conversation.
4. Memory for past events good.
5. Looks at books and pretends to read.
6. Likes recordings, words, and music that tell a story.
7. Enjoys counting objects.
8. Over 2,000 words in speaking vocabulary.
9. Can speak in complete sentences.

10. Can sing simple melodies, beat good rhythms, and recognize simple tunes.
11. Daydreams seem to center around make-believe play.
12. Attention span increasing up to 20 minutes in some cases.
13. Is able to plan activities.
14. Enjoys stories, dramatic play, and games.
15. Enjoys making up dances to music.
16. Pronunciation is usually clear.
17. Can express his needs well in words.

Characteristics of Six-Year-Old Children

Physical Characteristics

1. Boys' height, 44 to 48 inches; weight, 41 to 54 pounds; girls' height, 43 to 48 inches; weight, 40 to 53 pounds.
2. Growth is gradual in weight and height.
3. Good supply of energy.
4. Marked activity urge absorbs him in running, jumping, chasing, and dodging games.
5. Muscular control becoming more effective with large objects.
6. There is a noticeable change in the eye-hand behavior.
7. Legs lengthening rapidly.
8. Big muscles crave activity.

Social Characteristics

1. Self-centered and has need for praise.
2. Likes to be first.
3. Indifferent to sex distinction.
4. Enjoys group play when groups tend to be small.
5. Likes parties, but behavior may not always be acceptable to adults.
6. The majority enjoy school association and have a desire to learn.
7. Interested in conduct of his friends.
8. Boys like to fight and wrestle with peers to prove masculinity.
9. Shows an interest in group approval.

Emotional Characteristics

1. Restless and may have difficulty in making decisions.
2. Emotional pattern of anger may be difficult to control at times.

3. Behavior patterns may often be explosive and unpredictable.
4. Jealousy toward siblings at times; at other times takes pride in siblings.
5. Greatly excited by anything new.
6. Behavior becomes susceptible to shifts in direction, inwardly motivated and outwardly stimulated.
7. May be self-assertive and dramatic.

Intellectual Characteristics

1. Speaking vocabulary of over 2,500 words.
2. Interest span inclined to be short.
3. Can learn number combinations making up to ten.
4. Can learn comparative values of the common coins.
5. Can define simple objects in terms of what they are used for.
6. Can learn difference between right and left side of body.
7. Has an association with creative activity and motorized life experiences.
8. Drawings are crude but realistic and suggestive of early man.
9. Will contribute to guided group planning.
10. Conversation usually concerns his own experiences and interests.
11. Curiosity is active and memory is strong.
12. Identifies himself with imaginary characters.

Characteristics of Seven-Year-Old Children

Physical Characteristics

1. Boys' height, 46 to 51 inches; weight, 45 to 60 pounds; girls' height, 46 to 50 inches; weight, 44 to 59 pounds.
2. Big muscle activity predominates in interest and value.
3. More improvement in eye-hand coordination.
4. May grow 2 or 3 inches and gain 3 to 5 pounds in weight during the year.
5. Tires easily and shows fatigue in the afternoon.
6. Has slow reaction time.
7. Heart and lungs are smallest in proportion to body size.
8. General health may be precarious, with susceptibility to disease high and resistance low.
9. Endurance is relatively low.

10. Coordination is improving, with throwing and catching becoming more accurate.
11. Whole-body movements are under better control.
12. Small accessory muscles developing.
13. Displays amazing amounts of vitality.

Social Characteristics

1. Wants recognition for his individual achievements.
2. Sex differences are not of very great importance.
3. Not always a good loser.
4. Conversation often centers around family.
5. Learning to stand up for his own rights.
6. Interested in friends and is not influenced by their social or economic status.
7. May have nervous habits such as nail biting, tongue sucking, scratching, or pulling at ear.
8. Attaining orientation in time.
9. Shows greater signs of cooperative efforts.
10. Gets greater enjoyment from group play.

Emotional Characteristics

1. Curiosity and creative desires may condition responses.
2. May be difficult to take criticism from adults.
3. Wants to be more independent.
4. Reaching for new experiences and trying to relate himself to enlarged world.
5. Overanxious to reach goals set by parents and teachers.
6. Critical of himself and sensitive to failure.
7. Emotional pattern of anger is more controlled.
8. Becoming less impulsive and boisterous in actions than at six.

Intellectual Characteristics

1. Abstract thinking is barely beginning.
2. Is able to listen longer.
3. Reads some books by himself.
4. Is able to reason, but has little experience upon which to base judgments.
5. The attention span is still short and retention poor but does not object to repetition.

6. Reaction time is still slow.
7. Learning to evaluate the achievements of self and others.
8. Concerned with own lack of skill and achievement.
9. Becoming more realistic and less imaginative.

Characteristics of Eight-Year-Old Children

Physical Characteristics

1. Boys' height, 48 to 53 inches; weight, 49 to 70 pounds; girls' height, 48 to 52 inches; weight, 47 to 66 pounds.
2. Interested in games requiring coordination of small muscles.
3. Arms are lengthening and hands are growing larger.
4. Eyes can accommodate more easily.
5. Some develop poor posture.
6. Accidents appear to occur more frequently at this age.
7. Appreciates correct skill performance.

Social Characteristics

1. Girls may be more careful of their clothes than boys.
2. Leaves many things uncompleted.
3. Has special friends.
4. Has longer periods of peaceful play.
5. Does not like playing alone.
6. Enjoys dramatizing.
7. Starts collections.
8. Enjoys school and dislikes staying home.
9. Likes variety.
10. Recognition of property rights is well established.
11. Responds well to group activity.
12. Interest will focus on friends of own sex.
13. Beginning of the desire to become a member of the club.

Emotional Characteristics

1. Dislikes taking much criticism from adults.
2. Can give and take criticism in his own group.
3. May develop enemies.
4. Does not like to be treated as a child.
5. Has a marked sense of humor.

6. First impulse is to blame others.
7. Becoming more realistic and wants to find out for himself.

Intellectual Characteristics

1. Can tell day of month and year.
2. Voluntary attention span is increasing.
3. Interested in far-off places, and ways of communication now have real meaning.
4. Becoming more aware of adult world and his place in it.
5. Ready to tackle almost anything.
6. Shows a capacity for self-evaluation.
7. Likes to memorize.
8. Not always too good at telling time, but very much aware of it.

Characteristics of Nine-Year-Old Children

Physical Characteristics

1. Boys' height, 50 to 55 inches; weight, 55 to 74 pounds; girls' height, 50 to 54 inches; weight, 52 to 74 pounds.
2. Increasing strength in arms, hands and fingers.
3. Endurance improving.
4. Needs and enjoys much activity; boys like to shout, wrestle and tussle with each other.
5. A few girls near puberty.
6. Girls' growth maturity gaining over boys' up to two years.
7. Girls enjoy active group games but are usually less noisy and less full of spontaneous energy than boys.
8. Likely to slouch and assume unusual postures.
9. Eyes are much better developed and are able to accommodate to close work with less strain.
10. Needs ten to eleven hours sleep on the average; is a good sleeper, but often does not get enough sleep.
11. May tend to overexercise.
12. Sex differences appear in recreational activities.
13. Interested in own body and wants to have questions answered.

Social Characteristics

1. Wants to be like others, talk like others and look like them.
2. Girls are becoming more interested in their clothes.
3. Is generally a conformist and may be afraid of that which is different.
4. Able to be on his own.
5. Able to be fairly responsible and dependable.
6. Some firm and loyal friendships may develop.
7. Increasing development of qualities of leadership and followership.
8. Increasing interest in activities involving challenges and adventure.
9. Increasing participation in varied and organized group activities.

Emotional Characteristics

1. May sometimes be outspoken and critical of adults he knows, although he has a genuine fondness for them.
2. Responds best to adults who treat him as an individual and approach him in an adult way.
3. Likes recognition for what he has done and responds well to deserved praise.
4. Likely to be backward about public recognition but likes private praise.
5. Developing sympathy and loyalty to others.
6. Does not mind criticism or punishment if he thinks it is fair but is indignant if he thinks it is unfair.
7. Disdainful of danger to and safety of himself, which may be a result of increasing interest in activities involving challenges and adventure.

Intellectual Characteristics

1. Individual differences are clear and distinct.
2. Some real interests are beginning to develop.
3. Beginning to have a strong sense of right and wrong.
4. Understands explanations.
5. Interests are closer to ten- or eleven-year-olds than to seven- or eight-year-olds.
6. As soon as a project fails to hold interest, it may be dropped without further thought.
7. Attention span is greatly increased.

8. Seems to be guided best by a reason, simple and clear-cut, for a decision which needs to be made.
9. Ready to learn from occasional failure of his judgment as long as learning takes place in situations where failure will not have too serious consequences.
10. Able to make up own mind and come to decisions.
11. Marked reading disabilities begin to be more evident and may tend to influence the personality.
12. Range of interest in reading, in that many are great readers while others may be barely interested in books.
13. Will average between six and seven words per remark.

Characteristics of Ten-Year-Old Children

Physical Characteristics

1. Boys' height, 52 to 57 inches; weight, 59 to 82 pounds; girls' height, 52 to 57 inches; weight 57 to 83 pounds.
2. Individuality is well-defined and insights are more mature.
3. Stability in growth rate and stability of physiological processes.
4. Physically active and likes to rush around and be busy.
5. Before the onset of puberty there is usually a resting period or plateau during which the boy or girl does not appear to gain in either height or weight.
6. Interested in the development of more skills.
7. Reaction time is improving.
8. Muscular strength does not seem to keep pace with growth.
9. Refining and elaborating skill in the use of small muscles.

Social Characteristics

1. Begins to recognize the fallibility of adults.
2. Moving more into a peer-centered society.
3. Both boys and girls are amazingly self-dependent.
4. Self-reliance has grown, and at the same time intensified group feelings are required.
5. Divergence between the two sexes is widening.
6. Great team loyalties are developing.
7. Beginning to identify with one's social contemporaries of the same sex.

8. Relatively easy to appeal to his reason.
9. On the whole he has a fairly critical sense of justice.
10. Boys show their friendship with other boys by wrestling and jostling with each other, while girls walk around with arms around each other as friends.
11. Interest in people, in the community and in affairs of the world is keen.
12. Interested in social problems in an elementary way and likes to take part in discussions.

Emotional Characteristics

1. Increasing tendency to rebel against adult domination.
2. Capable of loyalties and hero worship, and he can inspire it in his schoolmates.
3. Can be readily inspired to group loyalties in his club organization.
4. Likes the sense of solidarity which comes from keeping a group secret as a member of a group.
5. Girls dramatize with paper dolls many life situations in whispered secrets or in outspoken dialogue.
6. Each sex has an increasing tendency to show lack of sympathy and understanding with the other.
7. Boys' and girls' behavior and interests becoming increasingly different.

Intellectual Characteristics

1. Works with executive speed and likes the challenge of arithmetic.
2. Shows a capacity to budget his time and energy.
3. Can attend to a visual task and at the same time maintain conversation.
4. Some become discouraged and may give up trying when unsuccessful.
5. The attention span has lengthened considerably, with the child able to listen to and follow directions and retain knowledge more easily.
6. Beginning understanding of real causal relations.
7. Making finer conceptual distinctions and thinking reflectively.
8. Developing a scientific attitude.
9. Better oriented with respect to time.
10. Ready to plan his day and accept responsibility for getting things done on time.

Characteristics of Eleven-Year-Old Children

Physical Characteristics

1. Boys' height, 53 to 58 inches; weight, 64 to 91 pounds; girls' height, 53 to 59 inches; weight, 64 to 95 pounds.
2. Marked changes in muscle system causing awkwardness and habits sometimes distressing to the child.
3. Shows fatigue more easily.
4. Some girls and a few boys suddenly show rapid growth and evidence of the approach of adolescence.
5. In general, this is a period of good health with fewer diseases and infections.
6. On the average girls may be taller and heavier than boys.
7. Uneven growth of different parts of the body.
8. Rapid growth may result in laziness of the lateral type of child, and fatigue and irritability of the linear type.
9. Willing to work hard at acquiring physical skills, and emphasis is on excellence of performance of physical feats.
10. Boys are more active and rough in games than girls.
11. Eye-hand coordination well developed.
12. Bodily growth is more rapid than heart growth, and lungs are not fully developed.
13. Boys develop greater power in shoulder girdle and muscles.

Social Characteristics

1. Internal guiding standards have been set up and, although guided by what is done by other children, he will modify his behavior in line with those standards already set up.
2. Does a number of socially acceptable things not because they are right or wrong.
3. Although obsessed by standards of peers, he is anxious for social approval from adults.
4. Need for social life companionship of children of own age.
5. Liking for organized games more and more prominent.
6. Girls are likely to be self-conscious in the presence of boys and are usually much more mature than boys.
7. Team spirit is very strong.
8. Boys' and girls' interests are not always the same and there may be some antagonism between the sexes.

9. Often engages in silly behavior, such as giggling and clowning.
10. Girls are more interested in social appearance than are boys.

Emotional Characteristics

1. If unskilled in group games and game skills, he may tend to withdraw.
2. Boys may be concerned if they feel they are underdeveloped.
3. May appear to be indifferent and uncooperative.
4. Moods change quickly.
5. Wants to grow up but may be afraid to leave childhood security behind.
6. Increase in self-direction and in a serious attitude toward work.
7. Need for approval to feel secure.
8. Beginning to have a fully developed idea of own importance.

Intellectual Characteristics

1. Increasing power of attention and abstract reasoning.
2. Able to maintain a longer period of intellectual activity between firsthand experiences.
3. Interested in scientific experiments and procedures.
4. Can carry on many individual intellectual responsibilities.
5. Able to discuss problems and to see different sides of questions.
6. May lack maturity of judgment.
7. Increased language facility.
8. Attention span is increasing, and concentration may be given to a task for a long period of time.
9. Level of aspiration has increased.
10. Growing in ability to use several facts to make a decision.
11. Insight into causal relationships is developing more and is manifested by many why and how questions.

Characteristics of Twelve-Year-Old Children

Physical Characteristics

1. Boys' height, 55 to 61 inches; weight, 70 to 101 pounds; girls' height, 56 to 62 inches; weight, 72 to 107 pounds.
2. Becoming more skillful in the use of small muscles.
3. May be relatively little body change in some cases.

4. Ten hours of sleep is considered average.
5. Heart rate at rest is between 80 and 90.

Social Characteristics

1. Increasing identification of self with other children of own sex.
2. Increasing recognition of fallibility of adults.
3. May see himself as a child and adults as adults.
4. Getting ready to make the difficult transition to adolescence.
5. Pressure is being placed on individual at this level to begin to assume adult responsibilities.

Emotional Characteristics

1. Beginning to develop a truer picture of morality.
2. Clearer understanding of real causal relations.
3. The process of sexual maturation involves structural and physiological changes with possible perplexing and disturbing emotional problems.
4. Personal appearance may become a source of great conflict, and learning to appreciate good grooming or the reverse may be prevalent.
5. May be very easily hurt when criticized or made the scapegoat.
6. Maladjustments may occur when there is not a harmonious relationship between child and adults.

Intellectual Characteristics

1. Learns more ways of studying and controlling the physical world.
2. The use of language (on many occasions his own vocabulary) to exchange ideas or for explanatory reasons.
3. More use of reflective thinking and greater ease of distinction.
4. Continuation in development of scientific approach.

Perhaps the best source of *needs* and *interests* of children is their physical, social, emotional and intellectual characteristics. Thus, the preceding information could serve as a general guide for adults in their attempts to deal with children's needs and interests.

GENDER DIFFERENCES IN EARLY SCHOOL SUCCESS

It is interesting to note that many people have been critical of the early school environment, particularly as far as boys are concerned. Some of these critics have gone so far as to say that young boys are being discriminated against in their early school years. Let us examine the premise.

We have already stated that a generally accepted description of the term *learning* is that it involves some sort of change in *behavior.* Many learning theorists maintain that behavior is a product of heredity and environment. Unquestionably, it is very apparent that environment plays a major role in determining one's behavior. Although man is controlled by his environment, we must remember that it is an environment largely of his own making. The issue here is whether or not an environment is provided that is best suited for learning for boys, at least at the early school grade levels.

While the school has no control over ancestry, it can, within certain limitations, exercise some degree of control over the kind of environment in which the learner must function. Generally speaking, it is doubtful that all schools have provided an environment that is most conducive to learning as far as young boys are concerned. In fact, many child development specialists have characterized the environment at the primary level of education as *feminized.*

The biological differences between boys and girls in this particular age range should be considered, and it is questionable whether educational planning has always taken these important differences into account. Over the years there has been an accumulation of evidence on this general subject appearing in the literature on child development, some of which will be summarized in the following discussion.

Due to certain male hormonal conditions, boys tend to be more aggressive, restless, and impatient. In addition, the male has more rugged bone and muscular structure and, as a consequence, greater strength than the female at all ages. Because of this, males tend to display greater muscular reactivity, which in turn expresses itself in a stronger tendency toward restlessness and vigorous overt activity. This condition is concerned with the greater oxygen consumption required to fulfill the male's need for increased energy production. The male organism might be compared to an engine that operates at higher levels of speed and intensity than the less energetic female organism. Several years ago, Doctor Franklin Henry of the University of California at Berkeley found in his research that, on average, males have what might be called an "active response set," whereas females might have a "reactive response set." This could be interpreted to mean that males confront the environment with an activity orientation, while females have a response orientation.

Another factor to take into account is the difference in basal metabolic rate (BMR) in young boys and girls. The BMR is indicative of the speed at which body fuel is changed to energy, as well as how fast this energy is used. The BMR can be measured in terms of calories per meter of heat energy in food. It has been found that, on average, BMR rises from birth to about three years of age and then starts to decline until the ages of approximately 20 to 24. The BMR is higher for boys than for girls, particularly at the early age levels. Because of the higher BMR, boys will in turn have a higher amount of energy to expend. Because of differences in sex hormone conditions and basal metabolic rate, it appears logical to assume that these factors will influence the male in his behavior patterns.

From a growth and development point of view, while at birth the female is from one-half to one centimeter less in length than the male and around 300 grams less in weight, she is actually a much better developed organism. It is estimated on the average that at the time of entrance into school, the female is usually six to twelve months more physically mature than the male. As a result, girls may be likely to learn earlier how to perform such tasks of manual dexterity as buttoning their clothing. In one of our own observational studies of preschool children it was found that little girls were able to perform the task of tying their shoelaces at a rate of almost four times that of little boys.

Although all schools should not be categorized in the same manner, many of them have been captured by the dead hand of tradition and ordinarily provide an environment that places emphasis upon such factors as neatness, orderliness, and passiveness, all of which are easier for girls to conform to than boys. Of course, this may be partly because our culture has forced females to be identified with many of these characteristics.

The authoritarian and sedentary classroom atmosphere that prevails in some schools and that involves the "sit still and listen" syndrome fails to take into account the greater activity drive and physical aggressiveness of boys. What have been characterized as feminization traits prevailing in many elementary schools tend to have an adverse influence on the young male child as far as learning is concerned.

Some studies show that as far as hyperactivity (overactive) is concerned, boys may outnumber girls by a ratio of as much as nine to one. This may be one of the reasons why teachers generally tend to rate young males as being so much more aggressive than females, with the result that young boys are considered to be more negative and introverted. Because of these characteristics, boys generally have poorer relationships with their teachers than do girls, and in the area of behavior problems and discipline boys account for twice as many disturbances as girls. The importance of this factor is borne out when it is considered that good teacher-pupil relationships tend to raise the achievement level of both sexes.

Various studies have shown that girls generally receive higher grades than boys even though boys may achieve as well as, and in some instances better than, girls. It is also clearly evident that boys in the early years fail twice as often as girls even when there is no significant difference between intelligence and achievement test scores of both sexes. This suggests that even though both sexes have the same intellectual tools, there are other factors that are against learning as far as boys are concerned.

If one is willing to accept the research findings and observational evidence appearing in the child development literature regarding the premise outlined here, then the question is: What attempts, if any, are being made to improve the condition? At one time it was thought that the solution might lie in the defeminization of the schools at the early age levels by putting more men into classrooms. This apparently has met with little success, because the learning environment remains essentially the same regardless of the gender of the teacher. Some educators have suggested that little boys start to school later or that little girls start earlier. The problem with this, of course, is that state laws concerned with school entrance are likely to distinguish only in terms of age and not gender. In a few remote instances some schools have experimented with separating boys and girls at the early grade levels. In some cases this form of grouping has resulted in both groups achieving at a higher level than when the sexes were in classes together.

The major question that must be posed is: What can be done to at least partially restructure an environment that will be more favorable to the learning of young boys? One step in this direction recommended by various child development specialists is to develop curriculum content that is more *action* oriented, thus taking into account the basic need for motor activity involved in human movement. Deep consideration might well be given to learning activities through which excess energy, especially of boys, can be used. One step in the implementation of this recommendation could be to give more consideration to the active play learning medium.

Lest the reader be concerned that we are recommending that children go to school to play all the time, we are not suggesting that the environment be restructured to include *only* this kind of procedure. However, it might well be considered, particularly at those times when young children, both boys and girls, become exceedingly restless in a sedentary learning situation. Thus, we are not advocating that this be the only procedure used but that some consideration be given to the natural urge for body movement as a way of learning, because it is so consistent with the developmental needs of children.

The above discussion is not intended to imply that the active play learning approach should be used only for young boys. Although our research shows that it may be more favorable for boys, at the same time it provides a very desirable medium of learning for girls in their early school years. The reader should also remember (and we want to point this out very forcefully) that the preceding discussion is based on the so-called average boy or girl. Obviously, because of individual differences in children, both boys and girls will possibly deviate from the standards reported here.

THE NATURE OF LEARNING

The learning process is complicated and complex, and the task of explaining it has occupied the attention of psychologists for many years. In recent years, this effort has been intensified and more about learning is being discovered almost daily. It is not our intent to try to go into depth on anything as complicated as the learning process. On the other hand, it will be our purpose to make some generalized statements about it as well as to consider certain conditions under which learning is best likely to take place. The reason for this is that, although it is not definitely known what happens when learning takes place, a great deal is known about conditions under which it can take place most effectively.

The word *learning* is used in many connections. For example, we speak of learning how to walk, how to speak, how to make a living, and how to feel about various things such as failing, aggressiveness, going to school, and so forth. As has been mentioned previously, whatever kind of learning one is concerned with, specialists seem to agree that it involves some kind of change in behavior. Obviously, our concern here is with changes in behavior that are brought about by child-adult relationships with particular reference to active play.

Just what does change in behavior mean? This is an extremely important question because it suggests that the child proceeds promptly to behave in a certain way as a result of a child-adult interaction in an active play situation. The word *behavior* can refer to improved understandings as reflected verbally and/or in writing. Thus, even though a child cannot always change his or her behavior in terms of practical performance and actually *do* what he or she has learned, the child can reflect greater understanding in written or spoken verbal behavior. Moreover, he or she can reflect it in contrived classroom situations where he or she is able to act as though the improved understandings were being carried into actual situations. Unfortunately, some teachers may not worry too much about changes in a child's behavior beyond what can be accomplished on a written test.

Some Principles of Learning Applied to Active Play

There are various basic facts about the nature of human beings of which modern educators are more aware than educators of the past. Essentially, these facts involve some of the fundamental aspects of the learning process, which all good teaching should take into account. Older ideas of teaching methods were based on the notion that the teacher was the sole authority in terms of what was best for children, and that children were expected to learn regardless of the conditions surrounding the learning situation. For the most part, modern teaching replaces the older concept with methods that are based on certain beliefs of educational psychology. Outgrowths of these beliefs emerge in the form of *principles of learning*. The following principles should provide important guidelines for teachers and others for arranging learning experiences for children, and they suggest how desirable learning can take place when the principles are satisfactorily applied to learning through active play.

1. **The child's own purposeful goals should guide his learning activities.** For a desirable learning situation to prevail, adults should consider certain features about purposeful goals that guide learning activities. Of utmost importance is that the goal must seem worthwhile to the child. This will involve such factors as interest, attention, and motivation. Fortunately, in the recommended activities in this book involving learning about reading through active play, interest, attention, and motivation are "built-in" qualities. Thus, the adult does not necessarily need to "arouse" the child with various kinds of extrinsic motivating devices.

2. **The child should be given sufficient freedom to create his own responses in the situation he faces.** This principle indicates that *problem solving* is a very important way of human learning and that the child will learn mainly only through experience, either direct or indirect. This implies that an adult should provide every opportunity for the child to use his own judgment in the various situations that arise in the active play experience.

3. **The child agrees to and acts upon the learnings that he considers of most value to him.** Children accept as most valuable those things which are of greatest interest to them. This principle implies in part, then, that there should be a satisfactory balance between *needs* and *interests* of children in their active play experiences. Although it is of extreme importance to consider the needs of children in developing experiences, an adult should keep in mind that their interest is needed if the most desirable learning is to take place.

4. **The child should be given the opportunity to share cooperatively in learning experiences with others under the guidance but not the control of the adult.** This principle is concerned with those active play experiences that involve several players. The point that should be emphasized here is that although learning is an individual matter, it can take place well in a group. This is to say that children learn individually but that socialization should be retained. This can be achieved even if there are only two members participating, the adult and the child.

5. **The adult should act as a guide who understands the child as a growing organism.** This principle indicates that the adult should consider learning as an evolving process and not just as instant behavior. If a teacher is to regard his or her teaching efforts in terms of guidance and direction of behavior that results in learning, wisdom must be displayed as to when to "step in and teach" and when to step aside and watch for further opportunities to guide and direct behavior. The application of

this principle precludes an approach that is adult dominated. In this regard, the adult could be guided by the old saying that "children should learn by monkeying and not by aping."

It is quite likely that adults will have good success in using the active play experiences recommended in this book if they attempt to apply the above principles. The main reason for this is that their efforts in helping children learn to read and improve their reading ability through active play will be in line with those conditions under which learning takes place most effectively.

Chapter 2

ABOUT READING

It has been suggested that the ability to read was not considered important for most laymen until sometime after Johann Gutenberg invented the printing press in the fifteenth century, and the Protestant Reformation with its emphasis on individual interpretation of the Bible. Until that time, reading was generally restricted to the clergy and certain members of the nobility.[1]

THE NATURE OF READING

Practically all of us learn to read but, of course, with varying degrees of proficiency. Yet, to define exactly what reading means is not an easy task. A part of the reason for this is that it means different things to different people. It has been suggested that the psychologist thinks of reading as a thought process. Those who deal in semantics, which is the study of meanings, think of reading as the graphic representation of speech. The linguist, one who specializes in speech and language, is concerned with the sounds of language and its written form. Finally, the sociologist is concerned with the interaction of reading and culture.

As will be seen later in the Chapter, reading is an aspect of communication. As such, reading becomes more than just being able to recognize a word on a printed page. To communicate, a meaning must be shared and the reader must be able to comprehend. Thus, one of the most important concerns in teaching reading is that of helping children develop comprehension skills.

Reading could be thought of as bringing meaning to the printed page instead of only gaining meaning *from* it. This means that the author of a reading selection does not necessarily convey ideas to the reader but stimulates him to construct them out of his own experience. (This is one of the major purposes of active play reading content which will be dealt with in detail in later chapters.)

---

1. The New Columbia Encyclopedia (New York, Columbia University Press, 4th ed., 1975), p. 2284.

31

Since reading is such a complex act and it cannot be easily defined, we will resort to a rather broad and comprehensive description of the term. Our description of reading is an *interpretation of written or printed verbal symbols.* This can range from graffiti on restroom walls to the Harvard Classics.

It should be borne in mind that the entire child reads; he reads with his senses, his experiences, his cultural heritage, and of course with his muscles. It is the latter aspect with which the present authors are predominantly concerned in this book, because the aspect of "muscle sense" involved in active play is an extremely important dimension in reading for children.

EYE MOVEMENTS IN READING

Early studies in reading focused on the visual act of reading as a means of better understanding of the process. Extensive research in this area continued through the 1940s. Such research resulted in the development of reading-eye cameras such as the Ophthalmograph (American Optical Company) by which eye movements could be recorded and analyzed.

From these studies the pattern of eye movements in the reading act is one of the eyes moving from left to right across the line of print with a return sweep to the next line, proceeding in a left-to-right direction again. This rhythmic movement line after line is broken by fixations as the eyes move across the line and regressions or backward movements.

At fixation points the eyes are not in motion. It is at this moment, however, that the vision is not blurred by movement and the visual act of reading takes place. The time of a "fixation" may vary from a third to a fourth of a second and is affected by the skill development of the reader and the difficulty of the material. Approximately 90 percent of the time spent in reading is accounted for by fixation points when the reader is going through the "seeing," the word-recognition, and the association process.

Regressions occur when there is a breakdown in the word-recognition and association aspects of the reading process. The reader may regress along the same line or several lines in order to arrive at word recognition or comprehension of the idea being presented. Some reading specialists caution that an excessive proportion of unknown words, inadequate experiences with the multiple meanings of words, and reading matter which is much too complex for the child's experiences all promote a faulty reading pattern and lack of progress in reading.

Eye span is another term used in describing the visual act. Eye span is the span of recognition during the moment of "fixation." For the elementary school child the eye span may be limited to the point where there is an average of two fixation points per word. The limitations of the eye span also indicates the demand upon the eyes in terms of the number of times the eyes converge in perfect alignment to focus at each "fixation."

As a visual task, adequate vision for reading calls for coordination and motility with accurate binocular shifts from point to point, accurate focus and accommodation to distance, a fine degree of parallel or coordinated action of both eyes and left-to-right directional attack.

When there is difficulty of function in eye movements this can result in loss of place, omissions, excessive repetitions, and slow rate. Defects in coordination, motility, directional attack, and form perception can prevent development of a desirable pattern of eye movement.

When there is evidence of deficiencies in visual perception or eye-hand coordination, developmental training can be given. Three major types of visual training for perception and discrimination are: (1) directionality, or orientation to direction, (2) ocular motility, or promoting coordinated movements of both eyes, and (3) form perception, or discrimination of similarities and differences in designs, figures, and word-like forms. (Some examples of how this training can be accomplished are presented in Chapter 4.)

WHEN TO BEGIN READING INSTRUCTION

Traditionally, the standard practice has been to begin the teaching of reading when children enter first grade at about six years of age. However, in recent years there appears to be a great deal of sentiment to start reading instruction before that time. A part of the reason for this is that there is a general feeling that young children are becoming more mature and possess more experience at an earlier age than was the case in the past. As a result of this prevailing belief, fully one-third of the teachers at the kindergarten level feel that their children can benefit from various forms of reading instruction. In fact, a large majority of kindergarten teachers conduct some of the fundamental phases of reading instruction, and only about 20 percent of them do *not* believe that reading instruction should be a part of the school program at that level.

A question that must be raised is: Does early reading instruction have any value? Completely solid evidence to support one position or another is lacking to make an unqualified valid conclusion. One very important consideration is whether or not early instruction benefits the child as far as his total development is concerned. Some child development specialists feel that such instruction, if too highly structured and formalized, can actually cause harm to some children as far as their emotional development and social adjustment are concerned.

It is important to mention at this point that education is as much the business of the home as of the school, because it is obvious that the school alone does not educate the child. Yet, many parents believe that a child begins to learn only when he enters school. They do not seem to realize that they are not only the child's first teacher but probably the most important one the child will ever have.

Parents can and should help prepare their children before they enter school and also assist their children with schoolwork after they are in school. An abundance of evidence is being accumulated to support this idea. For example, one national survey has shown that preschool children who have been "read to" by their parents perform better than those who do not receive such attention.

There are many valid reasons why this is true. Research in child development indicates that the direction of a child's mental development is likely to be determined between ten months and one and one-half years of age—and in some cases even lower. In addition, the human learning patterns can become well established by age three. Consequently, the action that parents take in helping their children is extremely important. Moreover, most authorities in the area of child development tend to feel that the first five years are the most important formative ones in the child's life. The child's ability to learn various skills in these formative years before he enters school may depend a good bit on the extent to which his parents provide him with desirable and worthwhile learning experiences.

It has been estimated that of the approximately three to four million children entering first grade, more than 400,000 of them will be asked to repeat that grade. It has been further estimated that if present trends continue, one-fourth of current first grade children, by the time they reach the age of eleven, will be reading two or more years below grade level. In fact, school officials of one large city system recently reported that about 50 percent of its students were dropping out of school at the ninth grade level because inability to read would prevent them from graduating from high school.

It is easy to blame the schools for this sad state of affairs. However, before doing so we might well take another look of the responsibility of parents as important helpers in the education of their children.

READING READINESS

Closely allied to the problem of when to begin reading instruction is the question of reading readiness. There are certain *developmental tasks* that are important for children to accomplish. Reading can be considered as such a developmental task. That is, it is a task that a child needs to perform to satisfy his personal needs as well as those requirements which society and the culture impose upon him. In viewing reading as a developmental task, we can then consider reading readiness as a developmental *stage* at which certain factors have prepared the child for reading.

At one time, reading readiness was considered only as being concerned with the child being ready to *begin* the reading experience. In more recent years it has come to be thought of more in terms of each step of reading as one concerned with readiness for further reading. Therefore, the idea of reading readiness is not confined only to the start of reading instruction but to the teaching and learning of most all reading skills. A given child may be considered ready to *learn to read* at a certain age. However, this same child may not necessarily be ready to *read to learn* until a later time. In fact, some reading specialists consider the primary level of grades one through three as a time for learning to read, and the intermediate level of grades four through six as a time when the child begins to read to learn.

Reading readiness needs to be thought of as a complex combination of basic abilities and conditions and not only as a single characteristic. This combination includes (1) various aspects of visual ability, (2) certain factors concerned with the auditory sense, (3) sex differences, (4) age, and (5) socioeconomic conditions. Obviously, it is not our purpose here to go into detail with reference to these various characteristics but merely to identify them at this point. In Chapter 5 some specific recommendations will be made concerning the application and function of active play as a medium for dealing with certain aspects of reading readiness.

SCHOOL READING PROGRAMS

One of the very important school curriculum areas in the education of young children is the *language arts* program. This program includes listening, speaking, reading and writing, all of which are concerned with communication. The primary purpose of the language arts program in the modern elementary school is to facilitate communication.

Speaking and writing can be referred to as the *expressive* phases of language, while listening and reading are considered the *receptive* phases. This implies that through speaking and writing the individual has the opportunity to express his or her own thoughts and feelings to others. Through reading and listening the individual receives the thoughts and feelings of others.

Although we have indicated that the language arts program contains listening, speaking, reading, and writing, the reader should not interpret this to mean that these are considered as entirely separate entities. On the contrary, they are closely interrelated, and each can be considered a component part of the broad area of communication. Such areas of study in the school as spelling, word meanings, and word recognition are involved in each of the four areas.

The importance of the interrelationship of the various language arts can be shown in different ways. For example, children must use words in speaking and have them meaningful before they can read them successfully. Also, they can spell better the words that they read with understanding and that they want to use for their own purposes. In addition, their handwriting even improves when they use it in purposeful and meaningful communication when someone they like is going to read it. Perhaps the two most closely interrelated and interdependent phases of the language arts are listening and reading. In fact, most reading specialists agree that learning to listen is the first step in learning to read. This relationship will be very apparent, particularly in the final four chapters of this book.

The modern elementary school gives a great deal of attention to this interrelationship of the various phases of the language arts. This is reflected in the way in which language experiences are being provided for children in the better-than-average elementary school. In the traditional elementary school it was a common practice to treat such aspects of the language arts as reading, writing and spelling as separate subjects. As a result, they became more or less isolated and unrelated entities, and their full potential as media of expression probably was never fully realized. In the modern elementary school, where children have more freedom of expression and, consequently, greater opportunity for self-expression, the approach to teaching language arts is one that relates the various language areas to particular areas of interest. All of the phases of language arts—listening, speaking, reading and writing—are thus used in the solution of problems in all curriculum areas. This procedure is primarily based upon the assumption that skill in communication should be developed in all of the activities engaged in by children.

We have already said that through reading the individual receives the thoughts and feelings of others; therefore, reading is considered a receptive phase of language. In this case the word *receptive* might well carry a figurative as well as purely literal meaning. Indeed, reading has been on the "receiving end" of a great deal of criticism during recent years. Perhaps more criticism has been directed at it than all of the other school subjects combined. Although it may be difficult to determine precisely why reading has suffered the brunt of attack, one could speculate that it might be because, in general, most people consider reading as the real test of learning. In fact, in the early days of American education, grade levels tended to be thought of as "readers": a child was said to be in the "first reader," "second reader," and so on.

In modern times a good bit of controversy involving reading seems to center around two general areas. First, there has been criticism of the various methods of teaching reading, and second, there has been some question regarding the validity of the principles upon which these methods are based. Perhaps because of individual differences, any method used in absolute form to the exclusion of all other methods would not meet the needs of all children. For this reason it seems logical to assume that the procedures or combination of procedures employed should be those which best meet the needs of an individual child or a particular group of children.

It is not our purpose to extol or criticize any of the past or present methods of teaching reading. Rather, the content of this book is intended to show how active play experiences can be used to assist the child in his or her efforts to read.

Whenever innovations in instruction are recommended there is always concern that these innovations are consistent with what is now known about child growth and development as well as principles of learning. This is rightly so. As these innovations are being tried, there must also be an evaluation of their effectiveness in terms of educational objectives. The subsequent chapters of this book will therefore focus upon the theoretical basis of the *physical* aspect of the total personality and learning to read, along with specific use of the active play learning medium in such areas of reading as teaching children to read, diagnosing reading readiness and reading ability, teaching reading skills, and active play reading content.

Despite recurring admonitions as to the dangers of trying the "new" simply to be able to be identified as having innovative and progressive programs, there pervades throughout the literature a sense of urgency for new approaches and materials, different and more effective uses of the old approaches and materials, adaptive combinations of the old and new — something different, something that will work better than what our current reading instruction programs are producing. Programs are looking for answers from both the old and the innovative. But the message of the program is that we must try and we must find answers.

Chapter 3

THEORY OF LEARNING
ABOUT READING THROUGH ACTIVE PLAY

The theory that there is a high degree of relationship between reading and participation in active play is by no means new. For example, the famous French educator and ecclesiastic, Francois Fénelon (1651–1715), is reputed to have once said that he had seen certain children who had learned to read while playing. Although we are not entirely sure what he meant, we are willing to speculate that his statement was an early indication that there is a high level of compatibility between reading and active play, and a possible forerunner of some of the things expounded in this book. In general, we are concerned with two broad aspects concerning the phenomenon of active play and reading: (1) how children can develop reading skills through active play and (2) the use of active play reading content as a means of helping children to learn to read and to improve their ability to read. Both of these broad areas will be dealt with in detail in subsequent chapters.

No question about it, throughout the ages the concept of learning through active play has been held in high esteem by many outstanding philosophers and educators. Such pronouncements extend over several centuries from Plato's assertion that "learning takes place best through play and play situations" to a modern twentieth statement by L. P. Jacks that "the discovery of the educational possibilities of the play side of life may be counted one of the greatest discoveries of the present day."

One of the main reasons for going into a rather detailed discussion of the theory of child learning through active play is based on the idea that some people tend to be skeptical about this approach to learning. Perhaps the reason for this is that so many individuals tend to associate learning only with work. They seem to feel that children can learn only when "bent over a book." We hope that the following discussions will help to dispel this notion.

As mentioned previously, one aspect of active play and reading is that this approach to learning is concerned with how children can develop skills in the basic area of reading while actively engaged in such active play experiences as active games, rhythmic play and stunt play. It is based on the theory that children, being predominantly movement oriented, will learn better when what might be arbitrarily called *academic* learning takes place through pleasurable physical activity; that is, when the *motor* component (active play) operates at a maximal level in skill development in reading that has been essentially oriented to *verbal* learning. This is *not* to say that active play learning and verbal learning are two mutually exclusive kinds of learning. It is recognized that in verbal learning, which involves almost complete abstract symbolic manipulations, there may be, among others, such motor components as tension, subvocal speech, and physiological changes in metabolism, which operate at a minimal level. It is also recognized that in active play where the learning is predominantly motor in nature, verbal learning is evident, although perhaps at a minimal level. For example, when a child learns through the active play medium, there is a certain amount of verbalization (talking) in developing a "muscle sense" concept of the particular active play experience that is to be used.

This procedure of learning through active play involves the selection of an activity such as an active game, stunt or rhythm, which is taught to the child and used as a learning activity for the development of a skill in reading. An attempt is made to arrange an active learning situation so that a fundamental intellectual skill is practiced or rehearsed in the course of participating in the active play experience. (Several examples of this are presented in Chapters 5 and 6.)

FACTORS WHICH FACILITATE
CHILD LEARNING THROUGH ACTIVE PLAY

During the early school years (and at ages six to eight particularly), it is likely that learning is limited frequently by a relatively short attention span rather than only by intellectual capabilities. Moreover, some children who do not appear to learn well in abstract terms can more readily grasp concepts when given an opportunity to use them in an applied manner. In view of the fact that the child is a creature of movement and also since he is likely to deal better in concrete rather than abstract terms, it would seem to follow naturally that the active play learning medium is well suited for him.

The above statement should not be interpreted to mean that the authors are suggesting that learning through active play experiences (motor learning) and passive learning experiences (verbal learning) are two different kinds of learning. The position is taken here that *learning is learning,* even though in the active play approach the motor component may be operating at a higher level than in most of the traditional types of learning activities.

The theory of learning accepted here is that learning takes place in terms of reorganization of the systems of perception (such as seeing and hearing) into a functional and integrated whole because of the result of certain stimuli. This implies, as mentioned in Chapter 1, that *problem solving* is a very desirable and worthwhile way of human learning. In an active play situation that is well planned, a great deal of consideration should be given to the built-in possibilities for learning in terms of problem solving. In this approach, opportunities abound for near-ideal teaching-learning situations because of the many problems to be solved. Using active games as an example, the following sample questions asked by children indicate that there is a great opportunity for reflective thinking, use of judgment and problem solving in this type of experience.

1. Why didn't I get to touch the ball more often?
2. How can we make it a better game?
3. Would two circles be better than one?
4. How can I learn to throw the ball better?

Another very important factor to consider with respect to the active play learning medium is that a considerable part of the learning of children is motor in character, with the child devoting a good portion of his attention to skills of a movement nature. Furthermore, learnings of a movement nature tend to use up a large amount of the young child's time and energy and are often associated with other learnings. In addition, it is well known by experienced classroom teachers at the primary level that the child's motor mechanism is active to the extent that it is almost impossible for him to remain for a very long period in a quiet state. To demand prolonged sedentary states of children is actually, in a sense, in defiance of a basic physiological principle. This is concerned with the child's basic metabolic rate, which was discussed in detail in Chapter 1.

The comments made thus far have alluded to some of the *general* aspects of the value of the active play learning medium. The ensuing discussions will focus more specifically upon what might be arbitrarily called *inherent facilitive factors* in the active play learning medium which are highly compatible with child learning. These factors are *motivation, proprioception* and *reinforcement,* all of which are somewhat interdependent and interrelated.

Motivation

Motivation can be thought of as something that causes a person to act. It is concerned with *why* people do certain things. What, how, when, and where a person does something is easy to determine. On the other hand, *why* one acts in a certain way is not so easy to observe. Thought of in these terms, motivation could be considered as something that gives direction to one's behavior.

For purposes of this discussion we should take into account *extrinsic* and *intrinsic* motivation. Extrinsic motivation can be described as applying incentives that are external to a given activity so that performance may be improved. Intrinsic motivation means that a given activity is exciting enough for a person to engage in it for the purpose of enjoyment derived from the activity itself.

Extrinsic motivation has been and continues to be used as a means of spurring individuals to achievement. This most often takes the form of various kinds of reward incentives. The main objection to this type of motivation is that it may tend to focus the learner's attention upon the reward rather than the learning task and the total learning situation.

People are motivated for different reasons. In general, the child is motivated when he discovers what seems to him to be a suitable reason for engaging in a certain activity. The most valid reason, of course, is that he sees a purpose for the activity and derives enjoyment from it. The child must feel that what he is doing is important and purposeful. When this occurs and the child gets the impression that he is being successful in a given situation, the motivation is within the activity (intrinsic motivation). It comes about naturally as a result of the child's interest in the activity. It is the premise here that active play learning contains this built-in ingredient so necessary to desirable and worthwhile learning.

The following discussions of this section of the chapter will be concerned with two aspects of motivation that are considered to be an important part of the active play learning medium. These are: (1) motivation in relation to *interest* and (2) motivation in relation to *knowledge of results*.

Motivation in Relation to Interest

It is important to have an understanding of the meaning of interest as well as an appreciation of how interests function as an aid to learning. Described simply, *interest* is a state of being, a way of reacting to a certain situation. *Interests* are those areas to which a child reacts with interest over an extended period of time.

It was stated in Chapter 1 (as a principle of learning) that a good condition for learning is a situation in which a child agrees with and acts upon the learnings that he considers of most value to him. This means that the child accepts as most valuable those things which are of greatest interest to him. To the very large majority of children, active play experiences are likely to be of the greatest *personal* value.

Under most circumstances a very high interest level is maintained in active play experiences simply because of the expectation of pleasure that children tend to associate with such activities. The structure of a learning activity is directly related to the length of time the learning act can be tolerated by the learner without loss of interest. Active play experiences by their very nature are more likely to be so structured than are many of the traditional learning activities.

Motivation in Relation to Knowledge of Results

Knowledge of results is also commonly referred to as *feedback.* It has been recognized for years that feedback is the process of providing the learner with information as to how accurate his reactions were. Psychologists usually refer to feedback as knowledge of various kinds that the performer received about his performance.

Many learning theorists agree that knowledge of results is the strongest, most important aspect controlling performance and learning and, further, that studies have repeatedly shown that there is no improvement without it, progressive improvement with it, and deterioration after its withdrawal. In fact, there appears to be a sufficient abundance of objective evidence that indicates that learning is usually more effective when one receives some immediate information on how he is progressing. It would appear rather obvious that such knowledge of results is an important aid to learning, because one would have little idea of which of his responses were correct. Some psychologists compare it to trying to learn a task while blindfolded.

The active play learning medium provides almost instant knowledge of results because the child can actually *see* and *feel* himself involved in the activity. He does not become the victim of a poorly constructed paper-and-pencil test, the results of which may have little or no meaning for him.

Proprioception

Earlier in this Chapter it was stated that the theory of learning accepted here is that learning takes place in terms of reorganization of the systems of perception into a functional and integrated whole as a result of certain stimuli. These systems of perception, or sensory processes as they are sometimes referred to, are ordinarily considered to consist of the senses of sight, hearing, touch, smell, and taste. Even though this point of view is convenient for most purposes, it no doubt greatly simplifies the ways by which information can be fed into the human organism. A number of sources of sensory input are overlooked, particularly the senses that enable the body to maintain its correct posture. In fact, the 60 to 70 pounds of muscle, which include over 600 in number, that are attached to the skeleton of the average-sized man could well be his most important sense organ.

Various estimates indicate that the visual sense brings us more than three-fourths of our knowledge. Therefore, it could be said with little reservation that man is *eye-minded*. However, one prominent physiologist, the late Doctor Arthur Steinhaus, has reported that a larger portion of the nervous system is devoted to receiving and integrating sensory input originating in the muscles and joint structures than is devoted to the eye and ear combined. In view of this, it could be contended that man is *muscle sense* minded.

The scientific term for muscle sense is *proprioception*. At the risk of becoming too technical, we nevertheless should mention that the *proprioceptors* are sensory nerve terminals that give information concerning movements and position of the body. A proprioceptive feedback mechanism is involved, which in a sense regulates movement. Since children are so movement oriented, it appears a reasonable speculation that proprioceptive feedback from the receptors of muscles, skin, and joints may contribute to learning when active play is used to develop skills in reading. The combination of the psychological factor of motivation and the physiological factor of proprioception inherent in the active play learning approach to learning has caused us to coin the term *motor*vation to describe this phenomenon.

Credence has been given to the old Chinese proverb that "one picture is worth a thousand words." Another Chinese proverb extends the dimension of the learning process: "I hear and I forget. I see and I remember. I do and I understand." In modern times we need to give consideration to the possibility of *muscle use* for learning as being worth a thousand pictures.

Reinforcement

In considering the relationship of active play learning to reinforcement theory, the meaning of reinforcement needs to be taken into account. An acceptable general description of reinforcement is that there is an increase in the efficiency of a response to a stimulus brought about by the concurrent action of another stimulus. A simple example of this would be when a teacher gives praise and encouragement when a child is engaged in a task. Generally, the same principle applies when athletes refer to the "home court advantage." That is, the home fans are present to spur them on. The basis for contending that active play learning is consistent with general reinforcement theory is that it reinforces attention to the learning task and learning behavior. It keeps the child involved in the learning activity, which is perhaps the major application for reinforcement procedures. Moreover, there is perhaps little in the way of human behavior that is not reinforced, or at least reinforcible, by feedback of some sort. The importance of muscle sense (proprioception) feedback has already been discussed in this particular regard.

In summarizing this discussion it would appear that active play learning generally establishes a more effective situation for learning for the following reasons.

1. The greater motivation of the child in the active play learning situation involves emphasis on those behaviors directly concerned with the learning activities.
2. The proprioceptive emphasis in active play learning involves a greater number of *responses* associated with and conditioned to learning stimuli.
3. The gratifying aspects of active play learning provide a generalized situation of *reinforcers* for learning.

EVIDENCE TO SUPPORT THE ACTIVE PLAY LEARNING THEORY

Any approach to learning should be based at least to some degree upon objective evidence produced by experimental research, and this is the subject of the final discussion in this chapter.

There are a number of acceptable ways of studying how behavioral changes take place in children. In this regard, over a period of years we have conducted numerous controlled studies concerned with the active play approach to learning. Our findings are suggestive enough to give rise to some interesting conclusions, which may be briefly summarized as follows.

1. In general, children tend to learn certain skills in reading better through the active play learning medium than through many of the traditional approaches.
2. The active play approach, while favorable to both boys and girls, appears to be more favorable for boys.
3. When *active* play learning experiences are compared to *passive* play learning experiences (such as card games and board games), the active play approach is shown to be more favorable for both boys and girls.
4. The active play approach appears to be more favorable for children with average and below average intelligence.
5. For children with higher levels of intelligence, it may be possible to introduce more advanced concepts at an earlier age through the active play learning medium.

In addition to the above scientific findings, the many successful experiences with the active play learning activities recommended in this book should encourage teachers and others to use the approach in an effort to help children learn about reading through pleasurable and enjoyable experiences.

Chapter 4

IMPROVING ABILITY TO LEARN ABOUT READING THROUGH COMPENSATORY ACTIVE PLAY

The term *compensatory* as it applies to education is not new, and over the years it has been used in a variety of ways. Possibly, its derivation dates back to mid-nineteenth century Denmark.[1] At that time, what was known as the "compensatory education of cripples" involved the teaching of boys and young men with certain physical impairments such skills as basketmaking and shoemaking. The purpose was to prepare people who had certain deformities to be able to make a living on their own.

In this country about the turn of the century it was reported that "by compensatory education for deformed children is meant any special training which will make amends for their physical shortcomings and convert little cripples into men and women better fitted in some one direction to cope with fellow-man in the struggle for life."[2]

In recent years in this country compensatory education has taken on a much different meaning. That is, it has been concerned essentially with "compensating" for an inadequate early education in some way, or for providing a better background for beginning schoolchildren who come from a low socioeconomic background. A case in point is the *Headstart* program that has been sponsored by the federal government.

Educators and psychologists in Great Britain have attached still a different meaning to compensatory education.[3] In this regard Morris and Whiting have indicated that the term compensatory education now being used tends to replace the former term *re-education.* They contend

---

1. The Education of Crippled Children, *American Physical Education Review,* Vol. III, No. 3 September 1898, pp. 190–191.

2. The Education of Crippled Children, *American Physical Education Review.*

3. Morris, P. R., and Whiting, H. T. A., *Motor Impairment and Compensatory Education* (Philadelphia, Lea & Febiger, 1971), p. 9.

that the term re-education was often misused when standing for compensatory education. Re-education implied educating again persons who had previously reached an educational level and who now, for some reason, did not exhibit behavior at a level of which they were previously capable. These authors assert that compensatory education implies an attempt to make good a deficiency in a person's earlier education.

It is from this source that the present authors derived the term *compensatory active play*. The rationale for this term is that ordinarily the attempts to improve a deficiency in one's earlier education is likely to take place through a pleasurable physical activity such as active play.

Compensatory active play attempts to correct various types of child learning disabilities which may stem from an impairment of the central nervous system and/or have their roots in certain social or emotional problems of children. This aspect of active play, most often through the medium of *perceptual-motor development,* involves the correction, or at least some degree of improvement, of certain motor deficiencies, especially those associated with fine motor coordination. What some specialists have identified as a *perceptual-motor deficit* syndrome is said to exist with certain neurologically handicapped children. An attempt may be made to correct or improve fine motor control problems through a carefully developed sequence of motor competencies which follow a definite hierarchy of development.

How, then, does one go about improving a child's *ability to learn?* In the first place, something needs to be known about those abilities that need to be improved for desirable and worthwhile learning to take place. Generally speaking, these abilities can be classified under the broad area of *perceptual-motor* abilities. To understand the meaning of perceptual motor we first need to define the terms *perception* and *motor* separately, and then derive a meaning when these two terms are combined.

Perception is concerned with how we obtain information through the senses and what we make of it. For purposes here, the term *motor* is concerned with the impulse of motion, resulting in a change of position through the various forms of body movement. When the two terms are put together (perceptual motor), the implication is an organization of the information received through one or more of the senses, with related voluntary motor responses.

The development of perceptual-motor abilities in children is referred to by some child development specialists as the process of providing "learning to learn" activities. This means improvement upon such perceptual-motor qualities as *body awareness, laterality* and *directionality* (sense of direction), *auditory* and *visual perception skills* and *kinesthetic* and *tactile perception skills.* A deficiency in one or more of these can detract from a child's ability to learn—especially ability to learn to read.

It is the function of this chapter to help teachers and others determine if such deficiencies exist, along with recommended compensatory active play experiences to help improve upon them. Even though a deficiency does not exist in any of these factors, the active play experiences suggested can still be used to sharpen and improve upon these skills, which are so important to learning.

IMPROVING BODY AWARENESS
THROUGH COMPENSATORY ACTIVE PLAY

As far as this subject is concerned, there are a number of terms that have been used by different sources to convey essentially the same meaning. Among others, these include body awareness, body schema, body image, body concept, body sense and body experience. Regardless of which term is used, they all are likely to be concerned with the ability of the child to distinguish the particular features of the body parts. The present authors prefer to use the term *body awareness* for this purpose.

Most child development specialists tend to agree that a child's knowledge of the names and function of the various body parts is a very important factor in the improvement of learning ability. For example, body awareness gives a child a better understanding of the space his body takes and the relationship of its parts.

It is doubtful that there are any absolutely foolproof methods of detecting problems of body awareness in children. The reason for this is that many things that are said to indicate body awareness problems can also be symptoms of other deficiencies. Nevertheless, teachers and others should be alert to detect certain possible deficiencies.

Generally speaking, there are two ways in which deficiencies concerned with body awareness might be detected. First, some deficiencies can be noticed, at least in part, by observing certain behaviors; second, there are some relatively simple diagnostic techniques that can be used to detect such deficiencies. The following generalized list contains examples of both of these possibilities and is presented to assist the reader in this particular regard.

1. One technique often used to diagnose possible problems of body awareness is to have children make a drawing of themselves. The main reason for this is to see if certain parts of the body are not included in the drawing. Since the child's interest in drawing a man dates from his earliest attempts to represent things symbolically, it is possible, through typical drawings of young children, to trace certain characteristic stages of perceptual development. It has also been found that the procedure of drawing a picture of himself assists in helping to detect if there is lack of body awareness.

2. Sometimes the child with a lack of body awareness may show tenseness in his movements. At the same time he may be unsure of his movements as he attempts to move the body segments (arm or leg).

3. If the child is instructed to move a body part such as placing one foot forward, he may direct his attention to the body part before making the movement; or, he may look at another child to observe the movement before he attempts to make the movement himself. (This could also be because of not understanding the instructions for the movement.)

4. When instructed to use one body part (arm), he may move the corresponding body part (other arm) when it is not necessary. For example, he may be asked to swing the right arm and may also start to swing the left arm at the same time.

5. In such activities as catching an object, the child may turn toward the object when it is not necessary. For example, when a beanbag thrown to him approaches close to the child, he may move forward with either side of the body rather than trying to catch the beanbag with his hands while both feet remain stationary.

Compensatory Active Play Experiences Involving Body Awareness

In general, it might be said that when a child is given the opportunity to use his body freely in active play experiences, an increase in body awareness occurs. More specifically, there are certain activities that can be used in helping children identify and understand the use of various body parts as well as the relationship of these parts. Over a period of time we have conducted a number of experiments to determine the effect of participating in certain compensatory active play experiences on body awareness. The following activities have proved to be very useful for this purpose.

Busy Bee

The leader and child stand facing each other. To begin with, the leader can be the *caller*. The leader makes calls such as "shoulder-to-shoulder," "toe-to-toe," or "hand-to-hand." As the calls are made, the leader and child go through the motions with each other. After a few calls, the leader calls out "Busy Bee!" and the two of them, the leader and the child, run to a point that was previously decided on. The idea is to see who can reach this point first. The activity continues with the child being the caller. When this activity is used with a group of children, the caller stands in the middle of the activity area and makes the calls. At the signal of "Busy Bee" all children try to find a new partner, and the caller also tries to find a partner. The child who does not find a partner can be the caller when the activity is played again.

To give the reader an idea of how such a compensatory active play activity can improve upon body awareness, we report here on an experiment using this particular activity with a group of several kindergarten children. Before the activity, the children were asked to draw a picture of themselves. Many did not know how to begin, and others omitted some of the major limbs in their drawings. After playing Busy Bee, the children were asked to again draw a picture of themselves. This time they were more successful. All of the drawings had bodies, heads, arms, and legs. Some of them had hands, feet, eyes, and ears. A few even had teeth and hair.

Mirrors

To start this activity, the leader can stand facing the child a short distance away. The leader goes through a variety of movements and the child tries to do exactly the same thing; that is, he acts as a mirror. The child and leader take turns being the leader. This can be done with several players by having them stand in line with the leader in front of them going through the different movements.

In this activity the child becomes aware of different body parts and movements as the leader makes the various movements. The leader should be alert to see how quickly the child is able to do the movements that are made.

Move Along

The child lies on his back on the floor. The leader gives a signal such as a clap of the hands, and the child moves his arms and legs in any way that he chooses. The leader then gives the name of a movement, such as "Move your legs like a bicycle," and then gives the signal to begin the movement. This same activity can be used with several players.

The leader should observe very closely to see how rapidly the child responds to the movements called. Also, if the activity is used with several players, the leader should observe to see if the child or other children are waiting to see what other children are going to do before making the correct movement.

Measuring Worm

The child extends his body along the floor in a straight line facing down. His weight is supported by his hands and toes. With arms and legs extended he takes very short steps until his feet are near his hands. He then moves ahead on his hands with very short "steps" until his body is extended again. He continues to do this for a specified distance.

It should be brought to the attention of the child how he is using his hands and feet to move along like a measuring worm. In discussing this activity with the child, the use of the body parts, hands, arms, feet and legs is mentioned. During the activity the leader can see how the child reacts to the directions. Sometimes children confuse hands and arms and feet and legs.

Squat Through

From a standing position the child assumes a squatting stance, placing the hands on the surface area to the outside of his legs with the palms flat and the fingers forward. This is count number 1. Switching the weight to the hands and arms, the child extends his legs sharply to the rear until the body is straight. The weight of the body is now on the hands and the balls of the feet. This is count number 2. On count number 3 the child returns to the squatting position, and on count number 4 the child returns to the erect standing position.

The child is able to see the function of certain body parts as the weight is shifted. After directions are given for the performance of the activity, the leader can notice how well they are followed with reference to the correct position of the body parts concerned.

Touch

In this activity the leader calls out body parts, which the child tries to touch with each other. Some calls could be "Touch your knee with your arm," "Touch you ankle with your hand." As can be seen, the possibilities are many. The leader can observe to see if the correct touches are made.

Run Under

A balloon or a beach ball can be used for this activity. The leader calls out a body part and throws the balloon or ball into the air. The child tries to run under the ball or balloon and have it touch the body part called out by the leader.

Everybody Goes

The child stands at one end of the activity area. The leader stands in the middle of the area facing the child. At the opposite end of the area there is a goal line. The activity is started with the following rhyme.

> Head, shoulders, knees and toes.
> Eyes, ears, mouth and nose.
> Off and running everybody goes.

On the last word "goes," the child tries to run to the other end without being tagged by the leader. The activity continues with the child and leader changing places. When several players are used, they stand in line at the end of the activity area, and the one selected to be "It" stands in the center. When they run to the goal line, all of those tagged become helpers of "It" and play continues.

As the rhyme is recited, the child (children) in the line does the following motions: head—place both hands on the head; shoulders—place both hands on the shoulders; knees—bend at the waist and place hands on knees; toes—bend on down and touch the toes and resume standing position; eyes—point to the eyes; mouth—point to the mouth; nose—point to the nose.

It is a good idea for the leader to recite the rhyme, as he or she can judge how fast this should be done. The more accomplished the child (children) becomes, the faster the rhyme can be recited, and the child or children can recite the rhyme in unison. When the activity is first used, the leader can observe how closely the child is reacting to what the rhyme says. It may be found that the child is having difficulty. Thus, the activity becomes a means of diagnosing a lack of body awareness. It will be noted that with practice a child will improve in response to the rhyme. A different form of movement can be substituted for *running;* that is, it can be "Off and skipping (hopping, jumping, etc) everybody goes."

Snowflakes

Creative activities are highly recommended on the basis that when a child is able to use his body freely, there is a strong likelihood that there will be increased body awareness. This creative activity and those that follow are intended for this purpose. The leader reads to the child, and then with various degree of guidance the child tries to depict the activity in the reading selection by creating his own responses. (See Chapter 9 for additional information about creative experiences.)

Snow Flakes

Snow!
Snowflakes fall.
They fall down.
Down, down, down.
Around and around.
They fall to the ground.
    Could you move like snowflakes?

Mr Snowman and Mr. Sun

See Mr. Snowman.
See Mr. Sun.
Mr. Snowman sees Mr. Sun.
Mr. Snowman is going.
Going, going, going.
Mr. Snowman is gone.
Be Mr. Snowman.
    Could you do like Mr. Snowman?

Tick, Tock

Listen to the clock.
It says, "Tick, Tock" as it keeps the time.
Would you like to play you are a clock?
This is the way.
Stand up.
Hold your hands.

Keep your arms straight.
Now keep time with the clock by swinging your arms.
Ready.
Swing your arms from side to side.
Swing them to the tick tock of the clock.

Can you keep time as you move from side to side?

Automobile

Pretend you are an automobile.
Hum like the engine.
Hmm! Hmm! HMM!
Your feet are the wheels.
Go like an automobile.
Hum as you go.

Can you hum while you go like an automobile?

In these activities the leader can carefully observe the movements of the child with reference to the body parts used in the creative activities. "Did you use your arms? Your legs?" and so on. If the leader desires, a drum or suitable recording can be used as accompaniment.

IMPROVING LATERALITY AND DIRECTIONALITY THROUGH COMPENSATORY ACTIVE PLAY

Laterality and directionality are concerned with distinction of the body sides and sense of direction. More specifically, laterality is an internal awareness of the left and right sides of the body in relation to the child himself. It is concerned with the child's knowledge of how each side of the body is used separately or together. Directionality is the projection into space of laterality; that is, the awareness of left and right, up and down, over and under, etc., in the world around the child. Stated in another way, directionality in space is the ability to project outside the body the laterality that the child has developed within himself.

The categories of laterality and directionality make up the broader classification of *directional awareness.* The development of this quality is most important, in that it is an essential element for reading.

In another frame of reference in some kinds of visual tasks requiring the use of one eye, there appears to be an eye preference. In reading, it is believed that one eye may lead or be dominant. In tasks where one eye is used and one hand is used, most people will use those on the same side of the body. This is to say that there is *lateral dominance.* In the case of those who use the left eye and right hand or the opposite of this, *mixed dominance* is said to exist. Some studies suggest that mixed dominance may have a negative effect on motor coordination, but perhaps just as many investigators report that this is not the case.

Masland and Cratty[4] have summarized the research on the relationship between handedness, brain dominance, and reading ability and characterize the research as voluminous, often contradictory, and most confusing. The following conclusions are based on their broad review of research.

1. It has not been demonstrated that laterality of hand or eye dominance or mixed dominance bear a direct relationship to poor reading.
2. There is a very low correlation between handedness or eyedness and brain dominance for language. There is no evidence that changing handedness will influence the lateralization of other functions.
3. There are neither theoretical nor empirical data to support efforts to change handedness or eyedness as a means of improving reading ability.

A condition often related to dominance as far as reading is concerned is that of *reversals.* One type of reversal (static) refers to a child seeing letters reversed such as *n* and *b* appearing as *u* and *d.* In another type (kinetic) the child may see the word *no* as *on.* At one time reversals were considered as possibly related to dominance. However, later studies tended to negate this earlier view. In relatively recent years studies tend to support the contention that problems of visual perception, spatial orientation, and recognition of form rather than dominance patterns result in children making reversals.

Since laterality and directionality are important aspects of body awareness, some of the methods of detecting deficiencies in body awareness mentioned earlier in the chapter also apply here. In addition, it may be noted that the child is inclined to use just the dominant side of the body. Also, confusion may result if the child is given directions for body movements that call for a specific direction in which he is to move. In

---

4. Masland, Richard L. and Cratty, Bryant, J., The Nature of the Reading Process, the Rational Non-educational Remedial Methods, Eloise O. Calkins, ed. *Reading Forum,* NIMDS Monograph No. 11, Department of Health and Human Services, Washington, DC.

activities that require a child to run to a given point, such as a base, he may tend to veer away from it. Or, he may not perceive the position of other children in a game and, as a consequence, may run into them frequently. These are factors that teachers and others can observe in children in their natural play environment or in other movements that they make.

Some specialists have indicated that they have had success with a specific test of laterality. This test is given on a 4-inch-wide walking board that is two feet in length. The child tries to walk forward, backward, and sideways, right and left and left to right, while attempting to maintain his balance. It is suggested that a child with a laterality problem will experience difficulty moving one of the ways sideward, ordinarily from left to right.

Compensatory Active Play Experiences
Involving Laterality and Directionality

Generally speaking, a relatively large number of active play experiences involve some aspects of lateralness, while a more moderate number are concerned with directionality. Some active play experiences involve *unilateral* movements, those performed with one side or part of the body. Many active play experiences provide for *bilateral* movement. This means that both sides or segments of the body are in motion at the same time in the same manner, as in catching a large ball with both hands. *Cross-lateral* movement is involved when segments of the body are used at the same time but in a different manner. In fielding a ground ball a child may catch it in one hand and trap it with the other. Many active play experiences are concerned with changing direction, which is likely to involve directionality. The compensatory active play experiences that follow have been selected because they contain certain experiences in laterality and/or directionality. Also, in some of the activities, these experiences are more pronounced and receive more emphasis than might be the case with certain other activities.

Zigzag Run

With the individual child the leader can set up various objects about four feet apart and have the child run around them, first to the left and then to the right and so on. This activity gives practice in changing direction as the child runs around the objects. The leader can closely observe how much difficulty is encountered in performing the task. With several players, children can be put into teams and the activity carried out in relay fashion.

Hit It

The leader and the child stand a short distance apart. The leader tosses an object such as a balloon or beach ball to the child. The idea is for the child to try to hit the object in the direction called out by the leader. If the leader calls out "left," the child tries to hit it to the left. If the leader calls out "down," the child tries to hit it downward. The leader can call out any direction desired. After a time the leader and child can change, with the child throwing the object to the leader and going through the same procedure.

Move Around

The leader and the child stand a short distance apart. The leader calls out directions in which the child is to move, such as "move to the right," "move forward," "move backward," and so on. After a time the leader and child change positions.

Catch the Cane (See the story, "Wilbur Woodchuck and His Cane," in Chapter 8.)

The leader stands a short distance away from the child and, with one finger, holds a stick (cane) upright. When the leader calls "Go," the cane is let go and is allowed to fall. The child tries to catch the cane before it drops to the surface area. Then the leader and child change places. This activity helps in the development of directionality, eye-hand coordination, and listening discrimination.

Ostrich Tag

The child and leader stand a short distance apart. To start with, the leader is "It." The leader tries to tag the child as the child tries to avoid being tagged. The child can protect himself by standing in ostrich fashion; that is, he may stand on one foot with his hands behind his back. The other leg is swung back and forth to help maintain balance. If the leader tags the child before he is in position or after he has moved, the child becomes "It." It can be more fun if there are several players in this activity.

Before the activity starts the leader can indicate to the child on which foot he is to stand. The leader can then take note if he is standing on the designated foot. The leader might also take note if the child is having difficulty in maintaining balance when standing on one foot.

Crab Walk (See the story, "A Strange Way to Walk," in Chapter 10.)

The child sits on the surface area with his knees bent and his hands on the surface area behind his hips. He raises his hips until his trunk is straight. In this position he walks forward and backward or to the side on his hands and feet.

The number of steps taken may be specified with reference to direction; that is, so many steps forward and so many backward. Also, the leader can call out the direction for the "crab" to pursue: forward, backward, or sideward left or right.

Up and Down

The child and leader stand facing each other holding hands. The child stoops down. When he stands the leader stoops down. They continue doing this. They can go up and down any number of times, calling out whether they are up or down.

Rocking Chair (See the story, "Rocking Chair," in Chapter 10.)

The child and leader sit on the surface area facing each other, with feet close to the body. Each can sit on the feet of the other or very close together. They grasp each other just above the elbows in this position and rock back and forth. They call out the words "forward" and "back" as they rock.

Log Roll

The child assumes a position on his stomach on a soft surface area such as a thick rug or mat. He extends his body by placing his arms over the head along the surface area. The arms are straight. The legs are also extended with the feet together and the toes pointed. The child then uses his head, shoulders, and hips to turn 360 degrees along the surface area. The child should attempt to roll in a straight line in either direction down the surface area. This is a good activity for developing directional movement. The leader should observe if the child is rolling in a straight line. This can be improved by keeping the body extended and straight. The child can call out his movements as he rolls first to one side and then to the other.

Go and Stop

This activity requires at least three players. They stand around the activity area, with one person designated as the *caller.* The caller points in a given direction and says "Hop that way." Or the caller may say "Skip to the wall." When the caller calls out "Stop," all of the players must stoop down. The idea is not to be the last one down. The last person has a point scored against him, and the activity continues for a specified amount of time.

In the early stages of this activity, it is a good idea for the leader to be the caller so he or she can control the various calls. The leader can observe if a child is unable to go immediately in the direction the leader specifies. The leader should be alert to see if a child watches another before making a movement. This can suggest whether a child is having difficulty in following directions.

Corn Race

This activity, which requires several players, is a modern version of a game that goes back into the history of our country. In early times while adults were husking corn, the children played games with the ears of corn. The players are divided into two or more rows. In front of each row a circle of about three feet in diameter is made on the playing area to represent a corn basket. Straight ahead beyond each of the corn baskets, four smaller circles are made about ten feet apart. In each of the four small circles is placed an object (a block, beanbag, etc.) representing an ear of corn. At a signal, the first child in each row runs to the small circles in front of and in line with his row, picks up the corn one ear at a time, and puts all the ears in the corn basket. The second child takes the ears from the corn basket and replaces them in the small circles, and the activity proceeds until all members have run and returned to their places.

This activity provides an opportunity to move forward and backward and to place objects in the process. The leader should take note if a child is confused about the particular task. Assistance can be given if a child needs it.

Change Circle Relay

This activity requires several players. The players are arranged in two or more rows. Three circles are made side by side on the surface area a given distance in front of each row. In the circle to the left of each row, three objects are placed. These objects can be anything that can be made to stand upright, such as cardboard milk cartons. The first child runs to the circle and moves the objects to the next circle; the second child moves them to the last circle, and then each succeeding child repeats this process; the objects are moved from the first circle to the second circle to the third circle and then back to the first circle. All of the objects must remain standing. If one falls, the last child to touch it must return and set it up. The activity is completed when all players in a row have had an opportunity to change the objects from one circle to another.

The number of objects can be varied, and the activity can be started with just one object. This activity gives children an opportunity to execute change in direction by placing objects in specified places. If the leader desires, the circles can be labeled with *left, center,* and *right.*

The Rhythm Game

Creative teachers can develop their own rhythmic activities and use movements that they desire. (See Chapter 9 for details about creative activities.) The following original verse, which indicates movements to be made, is an example.

> Point to the left.
> Now point to the right.
> Now turn around with all your might.
> Now take one step forward.
> Take one step back.
> Now try to be a jumping jack.
> Point your arms out.
> Point your toes in.
> Now give yourself a little spin.
> Now turn your head.
> Now bend your knees.
> Now buzz around like a hive of bees.

It is an interesting practice to have the child, with the guidance of the leader, also create experiences along the above lines. It has been our experience that activities of this nature are likely to be of extreme value because they are devised to meet the needs of a child or children in a specific situation.

IMPROVING THE FORMS OF PERCEPTION
THROUGH COMPENSATORY ACTIVE PLAY

At the beginning of this chapter we defined perception as how we obtain information through the senses and what we make of it. We should perhaps mention that this term is often defined differently by difference sources. Some sources describe perception as an individual's awareness of and reaction to stimuli. Others refer to it as the process by which the individual maintains contact with his environment. Still others describe it as the mental interpretation of messages received through the senses. While there are many descriptions of the term perception, it is likely that the reader will notice that these descriptions are more alike than they are different. Our description of perception tends to place the meaning of it in more or less simple terms.

Auditory Perception

It was estimated several years ago that about 75 percent of the waking hours are spent in verbal communication—45 percent in listening, 30 percent in speaking, 16 percent in reading, and the remaining 9 percent in writing. If this estimate is true, the importance of developing skills of listening cannot be denied. If children are going to learn effectively, care should be taken to improve upon their auditory perception—*the mental interpretation of what a person hears.* Without question, selective attention to sound is essential in helping children increase their effective use of auditory information. Moreover, by becoming a better listener and learning to ignore unrelated noise, the child can begin to hear important concepts needed to improve in reading. As will be seen in a subsequent chapter *from listening to reading* is a natural sequence.

Compensatory Active Play Experiences Involving Auditory Perception

Red Rover

The child stands at one end of the activity area, and the leader stands in the middle of the activity area. The area can be about 20 to 30 feet long and about 15 to 20 feet wide. The leader calls, "Red Rover, Red Rover let (name of child) come over." The child tries to run to the other end of the playing area before being tagged by the leader. The leader and child change places so that the child can have a turn at being the caller. The child must listen carefully and run at exactly the right time. This activity can be used with several players if desired.

Red Light

The leader and child take positions the same as for Red Rover, except that the leader has his or her back to the child. The leader calls out "Green light." At that signal the child starts to run to the other end of the playing area. At any time the leader can call out "Red light" and turn around to face the child. If the child is caught moving he must go back to the starting line. If not, the leader calls "Green light" again and the activity continues in this manner. The idea is for the child to get all the way to the goal line on the opposite end of the activity area. The child and leader should change places frequently so that the child can be the caller. The child must listen closely so as not to get caught moving when "Red light" is called. This activity can be used with several players if desired.

Clap and Move

The leader claps his or her hands using slow beats or fast beats. The child moves around the area to the sound of the hand claps. The child walks on the slow beat and runs on the fast beat. The child must be alert to respond to the different beats. After awhile the leader and child can exchange places.

Freeze and Melt

The child moves around the activity area in any way he chooses, such as walking, running, or hopping. When the leader calls out "Freeze," the child must stop. When the word "Melt" is called, the child begins to move around again. The child must listen very closely so as not to be caught moving when the word "Freeze" is called. After a time the leader and child can change places, with the child doing the calling.

Boiling Water

The child stands a short distance away from the leader holding a rubber ball. When the leader calls "Cold water," the child passes the ball to the leader. If the leader calls "Warm water," the child rolls the ball to the leader. If the leader calls "Boiling water," the child throws the ball into the air. The leader and child should change places frequently so that the child can be the caller. This activity can be used as a diagnostic technique to determine how well the child can distinguish auditory clues and perform the action required.

Stoop Tag

The child runs around the activity area saying, "I am happy! I am free! I am down! You can't catch me!" At the word "down" the child stoops down to avoid being tagged by the leader. If the child is tagged when not stooping, a point can be scored for the leader. The leader and child should change places frequently.

The child first learns to act on the basis of verbal instruction by others. In this regard it has been suggested that later he learns to guide and direct his own behavior on the basis of his own language activities—he talks to himself, giving himself instructions. In fact, speech as a form of communication between children and adults later becomes a means of organizing the child's own behavior. The function that was previously divided between two people—the child and adult—later becomes a function of human behavior. In this activity the child tells himself what to do and then does it. He says "I am down," then carries out this action.

Visual Perception

Visual perception can be defined as the *mental interpretation of what a person sees.* A number of aspects of visual perception have been identified, and children who have a deficiency in any of these may have difficulty with reading.

Various estimates indicate that the visual sense brings us upwards of three-fourths of our knowledge. If this is true, then certainly important consideration should be given to how well active play experiences can contribute to visual perception.

Compensatory Active Play Experiences Involving Visual Perception

The activities that follow are primarily concerned with *visualization* and *visual-motor coordination.* Visualization involves visual image, which is the mental reconstruction of visual experience, or the result of mentally combining a number of visual experiences. Visual-motor coordination is concerned with visual-motor tasks that involve the working together of vision and movement.

Hit the Balloon

The child is given a big balloon, and he tries to hit it as many times as he can with his hand before the balloon touches the ground. Other things that the child can do with the balloon is to hit it off a wall or hit the balloon back and forth with the leader or another child. This activity is good for eye-hand coordination.

Big Ball, Little Ball

The leader and child sit on the floor about ten feet from each other. One has a large ball such as a beach ball and the other has a smaller ball. The leader gives a signal and the big ball is rolled and the small ball is thrown. Both the leader and the child try to catch the ball, and the activity continues in this manner.

Ball Pass

This activity requires four or more players. The players are divided into two or more groups, and each group forms a small circle. The object is to pass a ball around the circle to see who can get it around first. The leader gives directions for the ball to be passed or tossed from one player to another. For example, the leader may say "Pass the ball to the right, toss the ball over two players," and so on. The activity may be varied by using several balls of different sizes and weights. This activity provides a good opportunity to improve eye-hand coordination, and it has been observed that after practice in this activity, poor coordination is likely to be improved.

Traffic Cop

The leader is the traffic cop and stands a given distance away from the child. The traffic cop carries a card, red on one side and green on the other. At the signal to go (green) from the traffic cop the child sees how far he can go before the stop signal (red) is given. If the child moves after the stop signal is given, he must go back to the original starting point. The leader and child can change places frequently.

Rather than using the colors, the words *Stop* and *Go* can be used on the cards so that the child can become familiar with the words as well as the colors. This activity helps the child coordinate movement with visual experience. It can also help the child become more adept at visual-motor association. The leader should be alert to observe if the child does not stop on signal.

Keep It Up

Depending upon the ability level of the child, a large rubber ball, a beach ball, or a large balloon can be used for this activity. On a signal the child tosses the ball into the air, and together the leader and child see how long they can keep it up without its touching the surface area. This is a good activity for the improvement of eye-hand coordination.

Kinesthetic Perception

Kinesthesis, the kinesthetic sense, has been described in many ways. Some definitions of the term are somewhat comprehensive, while others are less so. One comprehensive description of kinesthesis is that it is the sense which enables us to determine the position of the segments of the body, their rate, extent, and direction of movement, the position of the entire body, and the characteristics of total body motion. Another less complicated description of the term characterizes it as the sense that tells the individual where his body is and how it moves.

In summarizing the many definitions of the term, the following four factors seem to be constant, thus emphasizing the likenesses of the many definitions of the term: (1) position of the body segments, (2) precision of movement, (3) balance, and (4) space orientation. For our discussion here we will think of kinesthetic perception as the *mental interpretation of the sensation of body movement.*

Although there are a number of specific test items that are supposed to measure kinestheses, the use of such tests may be of questionable value in diagnosing the deficiencies in young children. Therefore, our recommendation is that teachers resort to the observation of certain behavior and mannerisms of children, using some simple diagnostic techniques to determine deficiencies in kinesthetic sensitivity.

Various authorities on the subject suggest that children with kinesthetic problems possess certain characteristics that may be identifying factors. For example, it has been indicated that a child who is deficient in kinesthetic sensitivity will likely be clumsy, awkward and inefficient in his movements and impaired in attempting to perform unfamiliar tasks involving body movement and can no doubt benefit from activities involving kinesthesis.

With reference to the above, teachers should be on the alert to observe a child who has difficulty with motor coordination; that is, using the muscles in such a manner that they work together effectively. Such lack of coordination may be seen in children who have difficulty in performing the movement skills that involve an uneven rhythm, such as *skipping*. Teachers can observe these deficiencies in the natural play activity of children, and a skill such as skipping can be used as a diagnostic technique in identifying such problems. (Skipping starts with a step and a hop on the same foot and can be taught from the walk. The push-off should be such a forceful upward one that the foot leaves the surface area. To maintain balance, a hop is taken. The sequence is step, push-off high, hop. The hop occurs on the same foot that was pushing off, and this is the skip. Some children will perform a variation of the skip around four years of age. With proper instruction, a majority of children should be able to accomplish this movement by age six.)

Since balance is an important aspect of kinestheses, simple tests for balance can be administered to determine if there is a lack of proficiency. One such test would be to have the child stand on either foot. Ordinarily, a child should be able to maintain such a position for a period of at least five seconds.

Compensatory Active Play Experiences Involving Kinesthetic Perception

Since kinesthetic sensitivity is concerned with the sensation of movement and orientation of the body in space, it is not an easy matter to isolate specific active play experiences suited *only* for this purpose. The reason for this, of course, is that practically all active play experiences involve total or near total physical response. Therefore, most active play experiences are of value in the improvement of kinesthetic sensitivity. However, the kinds of active play experiences that make the child particularly aware of the movement of certain muscle groups, as well as those where he encounters resistance, are of particular value in helping the child develop kinesthetic awareness of his body.

Rush and Pull

This activity requires a rope about 15 feet in length. The leader secures one end of the rope to an object. This object can be a chair or a bench and heavy enough to offer some resistance when the child pulls on the rope. The child should be able to pull the object, but at the same time it should not be too heavy for him to do so. The child stands a short distance away from the rope. On a signal the child runs to the rope and tries to pull the object. A game can be made out of the activity by such things as seeing how long it takes to pull the object a certain distance or simply pulling the object over a predetermined line.

In this activity the child experiences resistance as he tries to pull the object. He also experiences the feel of the muscle groups of the arms and legs working together.

Poison

This activity requires several players. The players form a circle and join hands. A circle is drawn on the activity area inside the circle of players and about 12 to 18 inches in front of the feet of the circle of players. With the hands joined, they pull and tug each other, trying to make one or more of the children step into the drawn circle. Anyone who steps into the circle is said to be "poisoned." As soon as a person is poisoned, someone calls out "Poison!" and the one who is poisoned becomes "It" and gives chase to the others. The other players run to various objects of certain material previously designated as *safety*, such as wood, stone, or metal. All of the players tagged are poisoned and become chasers. After those not tagged have reached safety, the leader calls out "Change!" and they must run to another safety point. Those tagged attempt to tag as many others as possible. The activity continues until all but one have been poisoned.

This activity provides an opportunity for kinesthetic awareness as a child tries to keep from being pulled into the circle. Also, surface area resistance may be encountered, depending upon the type of surface where the activity takes place.

Tactile Perception

The tactile sense is very closely related to the kinesthetic sense, so much so in fact that these two senses are often confused. One of the main reasons for this is that the ability to detect changes in touch (tactile) involves many of the same receptors concerned with informing the body of changes in its position. The essential difference between the tactile sense and the kinesthetic sense may be seen in the definitions of kinesthetic and tactile perception. As stated previously, kinesthetic perception involves the mental interpretation of the sensation of movement, whereas tactile perception is concerned with the *mental interpretation of what a person experiences through the sense of touch.*

Since the kinesthetic and tactile senses are so closely related, the identifying factors of deficiency in kinesthesis previously reported can also be used to determine if there is a deficiency in the tactile sense. Also, a number of elementary diagnostic techniques for tactile sensitivity can be played in a passive game type of situation so that the child is unaware of being tested. The following list suggests some representative examples, and creative teachers are limited only by their own imagination in expanding the list.

1. Have the child explore the surface and texture of objects around the room. Determine if he can differentiate among these objects.
2. Evaluate the child's experience by having him give the names of two or three hard objects, two or three rough objects, and so on.
3. Make a *touching box* by using an ordinary shoe box. Place several differently shaped objects and differently textured objects in the box. Have the child reach into the box without looking, and have him feel the various objects to see if he can identify them.

Compensatory Active Play Experiences Involving Tactile Perception

Children need tactile stimulation through touching and being touched. The following compensatory active play experiences, which involve touching and being touched, apply to tactile stimulation.

Touch Something

In this activity the child runs around the activity area and touches differently textured objects called out by the leader. For example, the leader can say "Touch something hard," "Touch something rough," etc. The idea is to see how quickly the child can react and make the touch on the correct object. After a time the child should be given the opportunity to be the caller.

Electric Shock

This activity requires about five or more players who form a circle, with one player designated as "It." The player who is "It" stands inside the circle and attempts to determine where the *electric power* is concentrated. The players in the circle join hands and one player is designated to start the electricity. This player accomplishes this by tightly squeezing the hand of the player on either side of him. As soon as a person's hand is squeezed, he keeps the electricity moving by squeezing the hand of the person next to him. If "It" thinks he knows where the electric power is (that is, whose hand is being squeezed), he calls out the person's name. If "It" has guessed correctly, all of the players in the circle run to a previously designated safety area to avoid being tagged by him. A point is scored against all of those tagged, and the activity continues with another player becoming "It." In this situation, the tactile sense becomes a medium of communication as each child's hand is squeezed by another.

Stunt Play

Certain stunts provide fine possibilities for tactile perception, in that some of them afford opportunities for body contact with others as well as with the surface area. A representative example of an activity requiring contact with the surface area follows.

SEAL CRAWL. (See story, "Sidney Seal," in Chapter 10.) In the Seal Crawl, the child supports himself on his hands while his body is extended back. The child squats and places his hands on the surface area shoulder-width apart, palms flat, and fingers pointed forward. He extends his legs in back of himself until his body is straight. The child points his toes so that a part of his weight will be on his hands, dragging his feet.

NOTE: Suggestions for conducting active games, rhythmic play and stunt play are presented in Chapters 8, 9, and 10.

Chapter 5

DIAGNOSIS OF READING READINESS
AND READING SKILLS THROUGH ACTIVE PLAY

A standard general description of the term *diagnosis* is the act of identifying a condition from its signs and symptoms. Applied to reading, diagnosis implies an analysis of reading behavior for purposes of discovering strengths and weaknesses of a child as a basis for more effective guidance of his reading efforts.

Among other things, it is important for us to try to discover why a child reads as he does, what he is able to read, and what he reads successfully. In addition, we need to know if he is having problems in reading, what these problems are, and the causes of the problems.

In the school situation many diagnostic tests are available for use and they have various degrees of validity. Studies tend to show that teachers themselves can forecast reading success of first grade children with about as much accuracy as reading readiness tests. It may be that such success in teacher observation has been a part of the reason for what is called *diagnostic teaching* becoming so important as school systems address their attention to meeting the needs of individual children.

CLASSROOM DIAGNOSIS

Over the years the term *diagnosis* has generally been thought of as a more formal out-of-classroom procedure for those children the teacher identifies as having difficulties in their attempts to learn to read. Occasionally, diagnosis is requested for those children whom teachers consider as not working up to their potential. More and more reading specialists are recognizing that in most cases classroom diagnosis can provide adequate information about the reading skill strengths and needs of children to help the classroom teacher make appropriate adjustments in instruction. Such adjustments involve focus on specific skills, levels of material, and method of instruction.

71

Classroom diagnosis has been directed to assessing the skill strengths and needs of children, either prior to or after instruction. Traditional measures have been standardized tests (usually of a survey nature), informal inventories, or teacher-made tests. The value of teacher observations of children during different types of reading situations has been recognized as essential to supplement information received from the traditional measures. Such observations are likely to be followed by recording and analyzing their reading performance.

The procedure of observing, recording, and analyzing a child's performance during the learning activity has come to be recognized as perhaps a more reliable assessment of his skills development. Such procedures have become the framework for diagnostic teaching. Two decades ago Guy L. Bond[1] gave a good description of diagnostic teaching: "It is based on an understanding of the *reading* strengths and needs of each child. These knowledges must be used to modify instructional procedures so that teaching, adjusted to the changing needs of the children, can be maintained. Such teaching is based on continuous diagnosis of the skill development of each child." It is at this point that the use of active play can have a unique role in diagnosis.

One of the many problems inherent in testing situations is the effect of a child's apprehension on his performance of the task involved. Basic principles of clinical diagnosis in reading have alluded to this problem by emphasizing the importance of establishing rapport with the child, starting the testing with less-threatening types of tasks, and stopping at the frustration level before complete discouragement disintegrates the testing situation. Teachers using such classroom diagnosis measures as mentioned often voice a concern relating to this apprehension on the part of children. They realize that the child must be put at ease as to the nature and the reason for testing. Paper-and-pencil tests throughout the grades, along with the aptitude tests and college entrance examinations, have resulted in adult aversion to test-taking to the point of significant blocking of what might be a usual performance level of an individual when not under stress.

---

1. Bond, Guy L., Diagnostic teaching in the classroom. In Deboer, Dorothy L. (Ed.): *Reading Diagnosis and Evaluation* (Newark, Delaware, International Reading Association, 1970), pp. 130–131.

Diagnostic Teaching Techniques

Diagnostic teaching techniques employing observation, recording, and analysis of children's performance in day-to-day reading situations has become a significant trend in assessment. Obtaining daily feedback is a key to structuring appropriate day-to-day learning activities, because they are based on the "real" reading performance of the child. It is a better "reading" of where the child is in his skills development. Therefore, in diagnostic teaching, teachers are using such techniques as coding errors made by children while oral reading to prove points in the discussion of material they are reading for a directed reading-thinking activity. In this way, the teacher has information about the children's sight vocabulary, word-attack application to unfamiliar words in context reading, and comprehension skills.

The every-pupil-response technique is used by the teacher as a diagnostic teaching procedure in many types of situations. With the technique calling for each child in a group to respond to a question or problem by holding up an answer card or signaling with a finger response a choice of answers, the teacher is able to check the performance of all the children. The teacher can observe each child's understanding and interpreting of the material, and his application of a specific skill to new words as in the case of reading. This technique not only provides information about each child's skills development within a group activity, but it also involves each child consistently throughout the learning and application of skills. This aspect of maximum involvement of each child within a group activity is particularly inherent in active play experiences. An example of this is the game "Match Cats," which is described later in the chapter.

It is interesting to note that these diagnostic techniques are geared to observing an individual child's performance within group learning activities. Teachers employing these techniques have reported they are better able to plan further activities for children to meet their individual needs through subgrouping children for additional learning experiences. As a result, the individualizing of instruction, a major objective of schools, becomes a reality.

Active Play as a Diagnostic Teaching Technique

By using active play experiences the use of children's naturally physically oriented world becomes a positive factor operating to facilitate further interest as well as more involvement and attending to the learning task. Many children tend to lose their apprehension of an intellectual task when it is "buried" in the context of an active play experience.

In particular, disabled readers will often perform tasks such as auditory and visual discrimination while engaging in an active play experience like "Man from Mars," "Match Cards" and "Letter Spot"[2] when they might be saying "I can't do it" in more traditional learning activities. Observations of children with severe reading problems, whose discouragement and frustration initially hampers their willingness even to participate, have found their natural affinity for physical activity has been the starting point of a more accurate assessment of their skill strengths and needs as well as remediation.

The total physical involvement of such children through active play experiences related to reading appears to act as a means for releasing the emotional blockage that inhibits any attempt to perform the intellectual reading tasks involved. And once these children participate successfully in such activities because of the strengthening of input through active play, the process of building more positive attitudes toward reading and a feeling that they can learn is begun. Needless to say, once the teacher has observed a higher-level performance of children in this setting, it is important to help the children recognize that they were able to, and did, perform the skill involved. Such children need to be shown they *can* and *have* mastered a skill with specific evidence that they have learned.

Four important factors in active play experiences that the teacher can utilize to determine whether further learning experiences are necessary for skill mastery are (1) the type of sensory input or modality involved in the reading task inherent in the active play experience, (2) the accuracy of the child's responses in the reading task, (3) the reaction time of children in performing that reading task, and (4) the self-evaluation of the child of his performance.

Sound instructional programs have always been specific-skill oriented. The impact of establishing behaviorally stated goals as objectives for instruction has helped teachers to move beyond such lesson plan goals as

---

2. Descriptions of these activities are presented later in this chapter.

"learning word-attack skills" to "being able to identify by name the initial letter of a word given orally" or "being able to give orally another word that begins with the same sound as a word presented visually." In the latter lesson objectives, both input and output modality are clearly stated so that a teacher observing such activities can analyze children's performance in regard to sensory modality both for input and output production. Such information helps the teacher to identify those children who consistently give evidence of significant differences in performance when lesson input is basically auditory or visual. Such information helps the teacher to adapt instruction accordingly and thereby assure more meaningful, and more successful, learning-to-read experiences.

Active play experiences related to reading by their very nature enable the teacher to identify the specific reading skills involved. The reading skills utilized in active play can be readily identified. An example of this would be the activity "Letter Spot" in which the reading skill is one of visual recognition of upper- and lowercase letters in order to play the activity. (This activity is explained later in the chapter.)

The second factor in the active play experience which a teacher can utilize is the accuracy of children's responses to the reading task inherent in the activity. It can be observed in those children who use the specific skill with at least 90 percent accuracy in their responses. This should represent skill mastery at the independent level. Any lower percentage of accuracy would indicate additional experiences are necessary.

The third factor relating to the reaction time of children's performance during the active play experience helps the teacher to identify the ease and comfort of children in performing a specific task. Reaction time in the present text refers to the amount of time it takes for the onset of a response of a person after receiving a stimulus. By observing the quickness of a child's response to the reading task inherent in the active play experience the teacher can assess the degree of ease as well as the accuracy of the child's responses. While percentage of accuracy is a useful and necessary tool in determining when a child reaches the point of skill mastery, the ease and comfort of the child during the reading task is also a significant factor. Skill mastery implies operation of an "automatic" level independently.

Of particular concern in consideration of reaction time are those children who have a disability in processing the sensory input with a resulting delay in reaction to the question or task presented. Such impairment can affect auditory, visual or feeling input. This may be related to the first factor in the use of active play as a diagnostic tool in which the teacher is observing children's performance in terms of modality used. In the activity "Call and Catch" (described later), the teacher adjusts the timing by momentarily holding the ball before throwing it into the air. In the case of reaction time there may simply be a lesser degree of impairment resulting only in more reaction time necessary to perform the task. The teacher must be aware that children may have this type of disability and attempt to recognize those children who consistently need additional time to respond to the task. It is important to adjust to the needs of such children rather than categorizing their delay in responding as being the result of disinterest or uncooperativeness. Active play experiences can easily be adapted to such children.

The fourth factor is that of self-evaluation by the children themselves. Children should be encouraged not only to react to the activity itself but also to assess how they did and what they might do to improve their performance of the reading skill involved. It might be a case of looking more carefully at the word, picture, or design cards used in the active play experience. In such pleasurable activities children appear more willing to examine their performance in the learning tasks involved, and quite realistically as well.

The uniqueness of active play, therefore, as another means of classroom diagnosis, is that such experiences tend to remove the apprehension of testing procedures and can demonstrate a level of skills development that is possibly more consistent with day-to-day performance. Such performance of the reading skill involved in the active play experience might even appear higher than when the children are engaged in more traditional reading activities. This higher level performance should then be taken as a more accurate assessment of children's potential level of performance when they are operating under optimum conditions of learning.

DIAGNOSING READING READINESS SKILLS
THROUGH ACTIVE PLAY

Reading readiness skills are a complex cluster of basic skills, including: (1) language development in which the child learns to transform *his experience* and *his environment* into language symbols through listening, oral language facility and a meaningful vocabulary; (2) the skills relating to the mechanics of reading such as left-to-right orientation, auditory and visual discrimination, and recognition of letter names and sounds; and (3) the cognitive processes of comparing, classifying, ordering, interpreting, summarizing, and imagining.

Likewise, sensorimotor skills provide a foundation for these basic skills by sharpening the senses and developing motor skills involving spatial, form, and time concepts. The following list identifies some concepts developed through direct body movement.

1. Body Awareness
2. Space and Direction
3. Balance
4. Basic Body Movements
5. Eye-Hand Coordination
6. Eye-Foot Coordination
7. Form Perception
8. Rhythm
9. Large Muscle Activity
10. Fine Muscle Activity

These skills are essential to the establishment of a sound foundation for the beginning-to-read experiences of children. Not only can the reading-readiness program, structured for the development of these skills, be facilitated through active play experiences, but diagnosis of progress in skills development can be obtained by teacher observation and children's self-evaluation. Active play experiences can be utilized effectively to provide meaningful and satisfying learning activities in the reading-readiness program. The following active play experiences are described to indicate the variety of activities that may be employed in the development and assessment of readiness skills.

Language Development

In such activities as the following, concept formation is translated into meaningful vocabulary.

CONCEPT: Classification

ACTIVITY: Pet Store

One fairly large Pet Store is marked off at one end of the activity area and a Home at the other end. At the side is a Cage. In the center of the playing area stands the Pet Store Owner. All the children stand in the Pet Store and are given a picture of one kind of pet (for example, fish, bird, dog). There should be about two or three pictures of each kind of pet. The Pet Store Owner calls "Fish" (or any of the other pets in the activity). The children who have pictures of fish must try to run from the Pet Store to their new Home without being caught or tagged by the Owner. If they are caught, they must go to the Cage and wait for the next call. The activity continues until all the Pets have tried to get to their new Home. Kinds of pets can be changed frequently.

APPLICATION: By grouping themselves according to the animal pictures, children are able to practice classifying things that swim, things that fly, and so forth. At the end of the activity the class can count how many fish, dogs, and so forth were caught. All the fish, birds, dogs, and so forth can then form their own line to *swim, fly* or *walk* back to the Pet Store, where new pictures can be given to the children for another game.

CONCEPT: Vocabulary Meaning—Action Words

ACTIVITY: What to Play

The children may stand beside their desks. One of the children is selected to be the leader. While that child is coming to the front of the room to lead, the rest of the class begins to sing:

> Mary tell us what to play,
> What to play, what to play,
> Mary tell us what to play,
> Tell us what to play.

(The song is sung to the tune of "Mary Had a Little Lamb.") The leader then says, "Let's play we're fishes," or "Let's wash dishes," or "Let's throw a ball." The leader then performs some action that the other children have to imitate. On a signal, the children stop and a new leader is selected.

APPLICATION: This activity gives children an opportunity to act out meanings of words. It helps them to recognize that spoken words represent actions of people as well as things that can be touched.

CONCEPT: Vocabulary Meaning—Left and Right

ACTIVITY: Changing Seats

Enough chairs for each child in the group are placed side by side in about four or five rows. The children sit alert, ready to move either way. The teacher calls, "Change right!" and each child moves into the seat to his right. When the teacher calls "Change left!" each child moves left. The child at the end of the row who does not have a seat to move to must run to the other end of the row to sit in the vacant seat there. The teacher can bring excitement to the activity by the quickness of commands or unexpectedness by calling the same direction several times in succession. After each command the first row of children who all find seats may score a point for that row.

APPLICATION: This type of activity makes children more aware of the necessity of differentiating left from right. At the beginning of the activity, children may not be able to differentiate directions rapidly. The teacher will need to gear the rapidity of his or her commands according to the skills of the group.

Auditory Discrimination

The following activity shows not only an active play experience using auditory discrimination skills but also the way activities can be adapted to other reading skills.

CONCEPT: Auditory Discrimination — Beginning Sounds of Words

ACTIVITY: Man from Mars

One child is selected to be the Man from Mars and stands in the center of the activity area. The other children stand behind a designated line at one end of the area. The activity begins when the children call out, "Man from Mars, can we chase him through the stars?" The teacher answers, "Yes, if your name begins like duck" (or any other word). All the children whose name begins with the same beginning sound as *duck*, or whatever word is called, chase the Man from Mars until he is caught. The child who tags him becomes the new Man from Mars and the activity continues.

APPLICATION: In order for the children to run at the right time, they must listen carefully and match beginning sounds. If the teacher sees a child not running when he should, individual help can be given. Children can also listen for words beginning like or ending like other words the teacher may use for the key word.

Visual Discrimination

The various activities described here relating to visual discrimination indicate the variety of active play situations which can be utilized to develop skills or to assess skills development.

CONCEPT: Visual Discrimination

ACTIVITY: Match Cats

The teacher makes duplicate sets of cards with pictures or designs on them with as many cards as there are children. The children sit on the surface area. The cards are passed out randomly. On a signal or music playing, the children move around the activity area with specified loco-motor movements such as hopping or skipping. When the music stops or a signal is given, each child finds the person with his duplicate card, joins one hand, and they sit down together. The last couple down becomes the Match Cats for that turn. The children then get up and exchange cards. The activity continues in the same manner with different locomotor movements used.

APPLICATION: Depending on the level of skills development of the children, the cards may be pictures of real objects or abstract forms, colors, alphabet letters, and words.

CONCEPT: Visual Discrimination

ACTIVITY: Mother May I (An Adaptation)

The children stand on a line at the back of the activity area. The teacher has cards showing object pairs, similar and different. The teacher holds up one pair of cards. If the paired objects or symbols are the same, the children may take one giant step forward. Any child who moves when he sees an unpaired set of cards must return to the starting line. The object of the activity is to reach the finish line on the opposite side of the playing area.

APPLICATION: The teacher may select cards to test any level of visual discrimination. Using pairs of cards for categorizing pictures would utilize concept and language development.

CONCEPT: Visual Discrimination

ACTIVITY: Match Cards

Each child in the group is given a different-colored card. Several children are given duplicate cards. There are two chairs placed in the center of the activity area. On a signal, the children may walk, skip, hop, etc., to the music around the activity area. When the music stops the teacher holds up a card. Those children whose cards match the teacher's card run to sit in the chairs. Anyone who got a seat scores a point. The play resumes. Cards should be exchanged frequently among the children.

APPLICATION: This visual discrimination activity can be adapted easily to include increasing complexity of the visual discrimination task as well as how the children move about and the task for scoring points.

Visual discrimination tasks might also include shapes, designs, letters (both uppercase and lowercase).

Letter Recognition

CONCEPT: Recognizing Letters of the Alphabet
ACTIVITY: Letter Spot

Pieces of paper with lowercase letters are placed in various spots around the activity area. There should be several pieces of paper with the same letters. The teacher has a number of large posters with the same but capital letters. (An overhead projector may be used to present letters in many letter styles, sizes, and colors.) A poster is shown to the class. The children must identify the letter by name and then run to that letter on the floor. Any child who is left without a spot gets a point against him. Any child who has less than five points at the end of the period is considered a winner.

APPLICATION: Children are helped to associate letters with their names. After the activity the posters can be put on display around the room.

CONCEPT: Recognizing Letters of the Alphabet
ACTIVITY: Call and Catch (variation)

The children stand in a circle. The teacher stands in the center of the circle with a rubber ball. Each child is assigned a different letter. The letter may be written on a card attached to a string which the child wears as a necklace. Each child reads his letter before the activity is started. The teacher calls out a letter and throws the ball into the air. The child who has that letter tries to catch the ball after it bounces. The teacher can provide for individual differences of children. For the slower child the teacher can call the letter and then momentarily hold the ball before throwing it into the air.

APPLICATION: This activity provides children the opportunity to become familiar with names and visual identification of letters. Later, the teacher could hold up letter cards rather than calling the letter. The children might then have to name the letter and catch the ball. Eventually, both upper- and lowercase cards might be used in the activity.

DIAGNOSING READING SKILLS THROUGH ACTIVE PLAY

As the child moves into the beginning reading skills, active play experiences continue to serve as a valuable means of assessing skill mastery. Skill areas as sight vocabulary, word-attack skills, alphabetical order, comprehension and vocabulary meaning can be developed through various dimensions of active play experiences. Likewise, level of skill mastery can also be assessed. Activities that utilize the various reading skills mentioned above are described in order to demonstrate the nature of active play experiences that can be employed.

Sight Vocabulary

Developing sight vocabulary through active play utilizes words and phrases from materials children are currently reading.

CONCEPT: Sight Vocabulary

ACTIVITY: Call Phrase

The children form a circle, facing the center. They may be seated or standing. One child is designated as the caller and stands in the center of the circle. Each child is given a card with a phrase printed on it. Several children can have the same phrase. The caller draws a card from a box containing corresponding phrase cards and holds up the card for every-one to see. When he reads the phrase, this is the signal for those children in the circle with the same phrase to exchange places before the caller can fill in one of the vacant places in the circle. The remaining child becomes the caller.

APPLICATION: Children need opportunities to develop quick recognition of phrases. This activity provides the repetition necessary to help children develop familiarity with phrases they are meeting in their reading material. The phrases may be taken from group experience stories, readers, or children's own experience stories.

Word Attack

Word-attack skills assessed through active play experiences may include phonic elements of words, rhyming words, vowel letter patterns, syllables, and endings.

CONCEPT: Auditory Discrimination—Consonant Digraphs (ch, sh, th)

ACTIVITY: Mouse and Cheese

A round mousetrap is formed by the children standing in a circle. In the center of the mousetrap is placed the cheese (a ball or some other object). The children are then assigned one of the consant digraphs *sh*, *ch*, or *th*. When the teacher calls a word beginning with a consonant digraph, all the children with this digraph run around the circle and back to their original place, representing the holes in the trap. Through these original places they run into the circle to get the cheese. The child who gets the cheese is the winning mouse for that turn. Another word is called, and the same procedure is followed. Children may be reassigned digraphs from time to time.

APPLICATION: Children need repetition for developing the ability to hear and identify various sound elements within words. This activity enables children to recognize consonant digraphs within the context of whole words. A variation of this activity would be to have the teacher hold up word cards with words beginning with consonant digraphs rather than saying the word. This variation would provide emphasis on visual discrimination of initial consonant digraphs. Another variation would focus on ending consonant digraphs, either auditory or visual recognition.

CONCEPT: Rhyming Words

ACTIVITY: Rhyme Chase

The children form a circle. Each child is given a card with a familiar word from the children's sight vocabulary written on it. The teacher may ask each child to pronounce his word before beginning the activity. The children should then listen and look at the words as each one identifies his word. The teacher then calls out a word that rhymes with one or several of the words held by the children. The child (or children) holds up his rhyming word so all the children can see it. He must then give another word that rhymes with his word. This is a signal for all the other children to run to a safety place previously designated by the teacher. The child (or children) with the rhyming words try to tag any one of the other children before he reaches a safe place. A child who is tagged receives a point. The object is for the children to get the lowest score possible. Word cards may be exchanged among the children after several turns.

APPLICATION: In this activity the children are called upon to relate auditory experiences in rhyming with visual presentations of these words. Sight vocabulary is also emphasized as the children reinforce the concept of visual patterns in rhyming words.

CONCEPT: Recognition of Visual Letter Patterns—Vowel Sound Principles (Open, Closed, Final *e*)

ACTIVITY: Letter Pattern Change

The children remain in their seats. Each child is given a card with a single-syllable word having one of the three vowel sound patterns (Examples: open-syllable pattern—a, he, go; closed-syllable pattern—get, bud, hip; final *e* pattern—game, lute, side). The teacher then holds up a word card with words also representing these patterns. Those children having words with the same letter pattern and the same vowel run to the chalkboard and write their word on the board and say it. Each child who is correct scores a point. Children may keep their own scores. Word cards should be changed frequently among the children. Later, the teacher may have the children whose word has the same letter pattern come to the board without it having to have the same vowel.

APPLICATION: The activity provides the children the opportunity to practice recognition of visual letter patterns as cues to vowel sounds. Children can be called upon to identify the name of the vowel sound principle that their word represents, for example, open, closed, or final *e.* The vowel digraph letter pattern might also be included in this activity.

Alphabetical Order

Alphabetizing words is an essential skill for locating words in dictionaries or information in encyclopedias. Active play experiences utilizing the first two, three or four letters for alphabetizing can later be developed as the teacher assesses when there is skill mastery of the less difficult tasks of alphabetizing.

CONCEPT: Alphabetical Order

ACTIVITY: Alphabet Lineup

The class is divided into teams. For each team a set of 26 cards, one for each letter of the alphabet, is placed out of order on the chalk tray at the front of the room or pinned to a bulletin board. The teams make rows at a specified distance from the letter display. A goal line is established at the back of the room for each team. The object of the activity is for each member, one at a time, to run to pick up a letter in correct alphabetical order, carry it to the team's goal line, and place the letter side by side in correct order. When each team member has found a letter, the team begins again until the alphabet is complete. The first team to complete placing the alphabet correctly at its goal line wins.

APPLICATION: Children need many different types of opportunity to practice putting the letters in correct alphabetical order. This activity provides a new way to practice this skill.

Comprehension

Vocabulary meaning[3] as well as other comprehension skills such as in the following active play experience utilizing sequence of events can be emphasized in active play. "Sentence Relay" further serves as an example of how the buddy system can work in the active play approach.

CONCEPT: Sequence of Events

ACTIVITY: Sentence Relay

Relay teams of five children each are selected to make rows before a starting line 10 to 15 feet from sentence charts for each team. The remaining children can serve as scorers. Each child on the team is given a sentence that fits into an overall sequence for the five sentences given a team. (The teams are given duplicate sentences.) Each sentence gives a clue to its position in the sentence sequence, either by idea content or word clue. On a given signal the team members get together and decide the correct sentence order. The child with the first sentence then runs to the sentence chart, places his sentence on the top line of the chart, underlines the key part of the sentence that gives the clue to the sequence, and returns to his team. The child with the next sentence then runs to place his sentence below the first sentence. This procedure continues until the sentences are in order. The team to complete the story with sentences in correct order first wins. The scorers check on the accuracy of the sentence order for each team. For the next game the scorers can exchange places with those who were on the teams. Variations of this activity can include the use of cartoons with each child being given one frame of the cartoon strip. To make the activity more difficult, more sentences may be added to the sequence. To prevent copying, the teacher can give different story sentences to each team.

APPLICATION: In this activity those children having difficulty with reading are helped by those who are more able readers and not eliminated from the activity. After the activity is played the teacher should go over key elements in the sentences that provided clues to the proper sequence.

How might "Sentence Relay" be used for diagnostic purposes? It might be used just as it is described above or certain adaptations might be made. In this case, the reading task in the active play experience is to recognize key elements in the sentences that provide clues to the proper

---

3. *What to Play* and *Changing Seats* are activities presented earlier in the chapter which reinforce vocabulary meaning.

sequence. The teacher can note whether a child is able to identify appropriate clues to sequence in his sentence. The teacher might observe which children perform the task easily and those who appear to need additional experiences in identifying key elements in sentences relating to sequence.

The activity might also be adapted by changing it to one that utilizes a story with several key sentences missing, the number of missing sentences being the same as the number of children on each team. The reading task would then be one of using context clues of a larger meaning unit to identify the proper order of sentences.

One of the many advantages of the active play approach is that it is fairly easy for the teacher to identify the specific reading skills being utilized in an activity which in turn facilitates assessment of children's mastery of that skill. In this way diagnostic teaching techniques aid a teacher's efforts to adjust the learning activities of the reading program to the needs of the children. The examples presented are representative of almost unlimited possibilities in structuring appropriate reading experiences for children. The creative teacher should be able to develop numerous activities by adapting those presented in the present text to the developmental level and skill needs of the children.

Chapter 6

DEVELOPING READING SKILLS THROUGH ACTIVE PLAY

The active play experiences in this chapter have been grouped by the major aspects of the reading program. Some of the activities are particularly useful for developing specific language or reading concepts. In these activities the learner acts out the concept and thus is able to visualize as well as get the *feel* of the concept. Other activities help to develop skills by using these skills in highly interesting and stimulating situations.

As in the previous chapter, the "Application" section for each activity indicates the appropriate use of this activity, whether for the development of a concept or for skill mastery.

Suggestions for adapting many of the activities are made in order to extend these types of activities to other elements of the various aspects of the reading program. The activities included have much versatility, depending on the creativeness of teachers and others using them.

The following illustration describes an active play experience one can use to help in the development of hearing and identifying syllables in words. This activity can be used to provide practice in recognizing one-syllable and two-syllable words. During and following the activity the teacher utilizes various aspects of the situation to see this relationship. The teacher's evaluation includes the children's reaction to the activity, how well they played it, and whether they developed the skill of hearing syllables in words from the activity.

CONCEPT: Syllabication

ACTIVITY: The Ocean is Stormy

Before going out to the activity area, the children should select the names of approximately six to ten fish having one-syllable names and six to ten fish having two-syllable names, depending on the size of the group. These names are written on the chalkboard and the children are asked to remember them. The children are then divided into couples

87

and proceed to the playing area. They group themselves by couples in the playing area, and circles are drawn around each couple except one. This extra couple is known as the Homeless Whales. The couples in the circles secretly select a name for themselves from the one-syllable fish names that had been written on the chalkboard. The Homeless Whales, holding hands, walk around the playing area and call out the name of a one-syllable fish. If their fish name is called, couples leave their circles, hold hands, and fall in line behind the Whales. All couples named must follow the Whales until the Whales suddenly call "The ocean is stormy." At this, all the couples trailing the Whales, and the Whales, run to an empty circle. The pair left without a circle become the Whales for the next game, and the former Whales choose a fish name. At any point in the activity the teacher may suddenly call "Typhoon," whereupon everyone, including those still standing in a circle, must seek a different circle. The next time the activity is played, children take names of fish with two syllables. Later, they may use three-syllable fish names. Children may have to use the encyclopedia to find fish with two or three syllables in their names.

Teaching Procedure:

TEACHER: Boys and girls, do you remember the other day we were studying about different kinds of animals? What are some of the kinds of animals that we learned about? (Children) Yes, one of the groups was fish. What were some of the characteristics of fish that we discussed? (Children) It was interesting to find out about some of the characteristics of fish. What were some of the names of the fish we read and talked about? (Children name fish, and the teacher writes the names on the chalkboard.) The other day we were finding out that words are divided into syllables. What did we say a syllable was? (Children) Yes, they are parts of a word. Dividing a word into syllables helps us to do what? (Children) Good. It is an aid to pronunciation, spelling and meaning. Let's look at the names of the fish we were just talking about and see if we can hear the parts of their names and divide them into syllables. (The children read the names of each fish on the list and decide how many syllables each one has.) Let's group the one-syllable fish names together. Tell me which ones belong in this list. (The teacher writes the names the children give.) Which names belong in a list of two-syllable fish names? (Children respond, and the teacher writes list.) Very good. Now let's say them once more so we will be able to remember them.

Today, we are going to play a game called "The Ocean Is Stormy." We are going to need to remember some of the one-syllable and two-syllable fish names in order to play our game. (The teacher goes over the procedures and answers any questions the children may have. The children move to the playing area and proceed with the game. During the game the teacher may make some comments.) Whales, make sure that you say the names of the fish loud enough so we can all hear you. You can also do things besides walk. You may run, skip, jump, or anything you choose. Whatever you do, the rest of the fish must follow. All right. Let's continue. (Children play the game.)

The activity continues for a time, and then the teacher evaluates with the class.

TEACHER: What did you like about The Ocean Is Stormy? (Children) Are you better able to remember the names of the fish? (Children) Are you better able to hear the number of syllables in the names of the fish? (Children) Do you think the game helped you to hear syllables in words? (Children) How can we improve our playing of The Ocean Is Stormy?

WORD ANALYSIS SKILLS

CONCEPT: Recognizing Letters of the Alphabet
ACTIVITY: Letter Snatch
The children are divided into two teams of eight to ten each. The teams face each other about ten to twelve feet apart. A small object such as an eraser is placed on the floor between the two teams. The members of both teams are given letters. The teacher then holds up a card with a letter on it. The children from each team who have the letter run out and try to grab the object and return to their line. If the child does so without being tagged by the other child, he scores two points. If he is tagged, the other team scores one point.

APPLICATION: Children have the opportunity to practice letter recognition in this activity. Visual matching can be with all small letters at first and then later with all capital letters. After the children have learned both small and capital letters, one team can have small letters and the other capital letters, with the teacher displaying cards showing either type of letter.

CONCEPT: Recognizing Letters of the Alphabet—Matching Capital and Small Letters

ACTIVITY: Large and Small

The children are divided into two teams of eight to ten each. The teams stand in lines about 15 feet apart and face in the same direction. The children on the first team are each given a card with a small letter on it. Each member of the second team is given a card with the corresponding capital letters. The members of the first team hold their cards behind them for the second team to be able to see. The teacher touches a child on the second team. This child then runs over to the first team, finds the child with the same letter as his, and tags the child. The child on the first team turns and chases the child who tagged him, who tries to get back into place before the other child touches him. If he is tagged, the first team gets one point; if he gets back safely, team two gets one point. After each child on the second team has had an opportunity to match his letter, the teacher then gives the children on the first team the opportunity to match the letters. To do this, the teams should both face in the opposite direction so that the first team can now see the letters the children on the second team hold behind their backs.

APPLICATION: This activity provides the necessary experience in associating capital and small letters that children need to become more familiar with the letters of the alphabet in upper- and lowercase form.

CONCEPT: Recognizing Letters of the Alphabet—Vowels

ACTIVITY: Magic Vowels

The playing area is considered the Magic Area. The vowels marked on it represent Magic Spots. The children make a single file and follow a leader around the area. When a stop signal is given, all those on Magic Spots are safe and score a point if they can name the vowel they are standing on. Those who are not standing on a Magic Spot or who cannot name the vowel do not score. The child with the most points wins.

APPLICATION: Children need opportunities to practice identification of the vowel letters. This activity provides the drill to aid in the recognition of the vowel letters. Children who are having difficulty are not eliminated from the activity and are thereby given the chance to continue practicing with the vowels until they become more familiar with them.

CONCEPT: Auditory Discrimination—Beginning Sounds in Words

ACTIVITY: Match the Sound

A group of eight to ten children form a circle. The children skip around in the circle until the teacher gives a signal to stop. The teacher then says a word and throws a ball directly at one of the children. The teacher begins to count to ten. The child who catches the ball must say another word which begins with the same sound before the teacher counts to ten. If the child does, he gets a point. The child with the most points wins. The other children in the circle must listen carefully to be sure each child calls out a correct word. As the children learn to associate letter names with sounds, the child must not only call another word beginning with the same sound but also must identify the letter that word begins with.

APPLICATION: This activity enables children to listen for sounds in the initial position of words. The activity can also be adapted to listening for final position sounds.

CONCEPT: Auditory Discrimination—Consonant Blends

ACTIVITY: Crows and Cranes

The playing area is divided by a center line. On opposite ends of the area are drawn base lines, parallel to the center line. The class is divided into two teams. The children of one team are designated as Crows and take position on one side of the play area, with the base line on their side of the center line serving as their safety zone. The members of the other team are designated as Cranes and take position on the other side of the play area, with their base line as a safety zone. The teacher stands to one side of the play area by the center line. The teacher then calls out "Cr-r-anes" or "Cr-r-ows." In calling cranes or crows, the teacher emphasizes the initial consonant blend. If the teacher calls the Crows, they turn and run to their base line to avoid being tagged. The Cranes attempt to tag their opponents before they can cross their baseline. The Cranes score a point for each Crow tagged. The Crows and Cranes then return to their places, and the teacher proceeds to call one of the groups; play continues in the same manner. This activity can be extended to include other words beginning with consonant blends, for example, swans and swallows, stork and starlings, squids and squabs.

APPLICATION: Repetition of the consonant blends during the activity helps children become aware of these sounds and to develop their auditory perception of the blends in the context of words. Discovering names of animals with other consonant blends can help children in their ability to hear consonant blends in the initial position of words.

CONCEPT: Auditory Discrimination—Consonant Blends

ACTIVITY: Call Blends

Eight to ten children stand in a circle. The teacher stands in the center of the circle, holding a ball. Each child is assigned an initial consonant blend by the teacher (st, gr, bl, cl, and so forth). When the teacher calls out a word with an initial consonant blend, the ball is thrown into the air. The child assigned that blend must then call a word using the blend and catch the ball after it has bounced once. Depending on the ability level of the children, the teacher can control the amount of time between calling out the blend word and the time the child catches the ball and calls out his word. When the child gives a correct word and catches the ball, he scores one point. The child with the most points wins. The teacher can reassign blends frequently to the children during the activity.

APPLICATION: This activity is a supplemental one to reinforce previous auditory and visual presentation of consonant blends in the initial position. Blends used in the activity should be those with which the children have worked. The teacher may write the word on the chalkboard after each time and have the child underline the blend in order to reinforce the blend in the visual context of the word.

CONCEPT: Auditory Discrimination—Final Consonant Blends (nk, ck, nd, st, nt, rst)

ACTIVITY: Final Blend Change

The children form a single circle, with one child standing in the center of the circle. The children in the circle are designated as different final consonant blends. Several children will be assigned the same blends. Each child may be given a card with his blend written on it to help him remember. The teacher then pronounces a word with one of the final position blends. All the children with this blend must hold up their card and then run to exchange places. The child in the center tries to get to one of the vacant places in the circle. The remaining child goes to the center.

APPLICATION: This activity helps children to develop their auditory discrimination of final position blends. They must listen carefully to the words pronounced. By holding up their card, they are associating the visual with the auditory symbol for that sound. The teacher may write the word down that is called out and have one of the children underline the final consonant blend so they can see the blend in the context of the whole word.

CONCEPT: Auditory Discrimination—Vowels

ACTIVITY: Build A Word

The children are divided into several teams. The teams stand in rows behind a starting line about 10 to 15 feet from the chalkboard. The teacher calls a word. The first child on each team runs to the board and writes another word with that vowel sound on the board. He then returns to his team and tags the next child. The second child then writes a second word with the same vowel sound on the board. If an error is made, the teacher helps the child correct it before the next child takes his turn. This procedure continues until every child has written a word on the board. The team finishing first scores a point. Another word is then called.

APPLICATION: This activity can be played when children have been introduced to vowel sounds, either a few or all of them. Words called by the teacher reflect those vowels which the children have been practicing. Words can be called using only the short sounds of all the vowels, then the long sounds of all the vowels, then both long and short sounds of one vowel, and finally long and short sounds of all vowels. This activity can be adapted to practicing with initial and final consonants.

CONCEPT: Rhyming Words

ACTIVITY: Rhyme Grab

The class is divided into two teams. The teams line up and face each other about 15 to 20 feet apart. A ball or beanbag is placed in the center of the area between the two teams. The members of each team are given corresponding rhyming words. The teacher calls a word. The children who have words that rhyme with the one the teacher calls try to snatch the ball. The child who gets the ball scores a point for his team. The team with the most points wins.

APPLICATION: Children need to have many situations that call upon their auditory skill in hearing words that rhyme. In this activity, children may also be given an opportunity to associate printed words with spoken words by having the teacher alternate holding up word cards and the children determining if the word assigned them rhymes with the printed word, or giving the children word cards and the teacher calling out words.

CONCEPT: Initial Consonant Substitution

ACTIVITY: First Letter Change

The class is divided into several teams. The teams stand in rows behind a starting line some 10 to 15 feet from the chalkboard. A word such as *ball* is written on the board for each team. (To prevent copying, different words should be used for each team.) On a signal the first child on each team goes to the board, says the word, writes another word, changing the initial consonant to make another meaningful word, says the word, and then runs to the rear of his team. The second child of the team repeats this same sequence. The first team to complete the writing of the words with initial consonant substitution correctly scores a point. Any child having trouble may ask the help of one member of his team to identify another word.

APPLICATION: Children are able to develop their skills in using initial consonant substitution in this activity with the added dimension of visual and kinesthetic experiences by seeing a word and writing new words, using different initial consonants.

CONCEPT: Visual Discrimination—Whole Words

ACTIVITY: See the Same

The children are divided into two groups. Sets of word cards are made up and placed in a large, shallow box, one for each team. The words selected are those being developed as sight vocabulary. A pair of word cards is made up for each word. The words are then mixed up in the boxes. The two teams stand in rows behind a starting line. On a signal the first child of each group runs to the group's box and looks for two words that are alike. He then displays the pair of words on a sentence chart holder that is set up next to the group's box. The next child in the group proceeds in the same manner. The first group who has each child find a pair of words wins. A child having difficulty may seek the help from one member of his group.

APPLICATION: Children need opportunities to visually match not only letters but also words in order for them to develop skills of seeing letter elements within the whole word. This activity provides an interesting means for developing this skill. The teacher may encourage the children to identify the word pair they have found. (If there are additional sentence chart holders, it is desirable to have smaller groups and thus more teams.)

CONCEPT: Visual Discrimination—Whole Words

ACTIVITY: Cross the Bridge

The activity area is marked off with lines at each end. A child is selected to be the Bridge Keeper. He stands in the center of the area while the remainder of the class stands behind one end line. Each child is given a card with a sight vocabulary word on it. Several children should have the same word. The Bridge Keeper is given a box with a complete set of word cards that correspond to those given the other children and large enough for all children to see. The children call out to the Bridge Keeper, "May we use the bridge? May we use the bridge?" The Bridge Keeper replies, "Yes, if you are this word." He then holds up one of the word cards from his box for all the children to see. The child or children having that word try to cross to the other end line without being tagged by the Bridge Keeper. The procedure is continued again with other words. Those children tagged must help the Bridge Keeper to tag other children as they also try to cross the bridge. Occasionally, the Bridge Keeper may call out, "Everybody across the Bridge," when all the children may then run to the opposite end line. The activity can continue until one child remains. He becomes the Bridge Keeper for the next time, or another Bridge Keeper may be selected.

APPLICATION: This activity provides children the opportunity to match words visually as a means to reinforce words to the point that they may become a part of the child's sight vocabulary.

CONCEPT: Auditory and Visual Association—Initial Consonants

ACTIVITY: Consonant Relay

The children are divided into several relay teams. The teams are a specific distance from the chalkboard and are seated. The teacher stands so as to be seen by the children when pronouncing the words. The teacher says a word beginning with a consonant sound. The last child on each team runs to the board, writes the beginning consonant, and returns to the head of his team. Each child moves back one place. The first child to get back to his seat with the correct letter written on the board scores a point for his team. The teacher says another word, and the activity continues as above until everyone has had a turn. The team with the highest score wins.

APPLICATION: This activity gives children practice in hearing initial consonant sounds and associating them with their written symbols. The activity can be adapted to working with final consonants, digraphs, blends, and long and short vowel sounds.

CONCEPT: Plurals of Nouns

ACTIVITY: Plural Relay

The class is divided into teams which stand in rows 10 to 15 feet from the chalkboard. Each team has a different list of nouns placed on the board. On a signal the first child runs to the board and writes the plural of the first noun next to it. He returns to the rear of his team, and the second child runs to the board and writes the plural of the second noun, and so on. The child who is having difficulty may call upon one of the members of his team to help him. The team that finishes first with all the plurals written correctly wins. At first, lists of nouns may just include regular plurals; later, words with irregular noun plurals may be added.

APPLICATION: This activity enables children to practice their skills in identifying plural forms of nouns. As irregular noun plurals are worked with, the children can be helped to note that not all nouns have the same plural endings. They can be helped to note that some nouns form their plurals by changing their spelling and that some nouns remain the same for the plural form.

CONCEPT: Inflectional Endings—*s, ed, ing*

ACTIVITY: Ending Relay

The class is divided into teams. Each team is given a box filled with sight vocabulary words having *s, ed,* and *ing* endings. The boxes are placed by the chalkboard. The teams make rows at a starting line 10 to 15 feet from the chalkboard. On a signal the first child of each team runs to the team's box and picks out three words, one with an *s* ending, one with *ed,* and one with an *ing* ending. He places the words along the chalk tray, pronounces each and returns to his team. The second child continues in the same manner. If a child is having difficulty, he may call upon one member of his team to help him. The team that finishes with the accurate selection and pronunciation of words first wins.

APPLICATION: This activity enables children to practice their skills in identifying visually presented words with different inflectional endings. The activity may later include words with irregular endings. It also provides reinforcement of sight vocabulary.

CONCEPT: Dividing Words Into Syllables

ACTIVITY: Syllable Relay

The children are divided into two teams. A captain is chosen for each team. The teams stand about 15 feet from a finish line. Each team is given a set of cards that have individual letters written on them. Each captain is given a red card. The teacher holds up a card with a two-syllable word written on it large enough for all to see. If the two-syllable word contains five letters, the first five children on each team look for the correct letters in their set of cards, run to the finish line, and stand, holding their letters in correct order to spell the word. The captain then stands with his red card between the letters where the word is divided into syllables. The team making up the word with the proper designation for dividing it into syllables first scores a point. The next word is then given. The next group of children on the team finds the necessary letters and proceeds in the same manner. The team with the highest score wins.

APPLICATION: When children have had some experience with syllabication rules (vc/cv, v/cv, and v/cle), this activity can provide the necessary drill for reinforcing these rules. Those children having difficulty can be helped to see the vowel-consonant patterns in the words as they group themselves as letters and how the words are divided into syllables. In this activity the children having difficulty are helped by other members of the team rather than being eliminated.

CONCEPT: Accent as Clues to Meaning

ACTIVITY: Accent Relay

The class is divided into several teams. The teams make rows behind a starting line 10 to 15 feet from the chalkboard. Complete sets of words (a few more than the number of children on the teams), divided into syllables and marked with accents, are written on the board. Examples of words to be used are *ob'ject* and *object'*, *re'cord* and *record'*. The teacher reads a sentence in which one of the words from the board is used. The first child on each team runs to the board and underlines the correct word as it was used in the teacher's sentence. He then returns to the rear of his team. The first child to return to his team scores a point for his team. The second child proceeds to underline a second word with the teacher's reading of another sentence. This procedure continues until each child has had an opportunity to participate. The team with the most points wins. At any time a child is having difficulty, he may ask one member of his team for help.

APPLICATION: This activity helps children to listen carefully to words in the context of a sentence for clues to meaning. Children can also be helped to note the change of the function of these words in sentences when there is an accent change, that of moving from a noun to a verb function.

CONCEPT: Alphabetical Order

ACTIVITY: Alphabet Relay

The children are divided into several teams. Word lists are written on the chalkboard for each team with as many words as there are team members. There should be different words in each list. The teams make rows behind a starting line 10 to 15 feet from the board. On a signal the first child on each team runs to the board and writes the number 1 in front of the first word in alphabetical order. Upon returning to the rear of his team, the second child runs and puts number 2 in front of the second word to come in alphabetical order. This procedure is continued until all the words are numbered in proper alphabetical order. The first team completing its list correctly wins. The difficulty of the alphabetizing task can be increased by using words with the same first letter, and so on. A child who is having difficulty may seek the help from one member of his team.

APPLICATION: This highly motivating activity provides children with the necessary repetition for developing skills of alphabetizing words. The nature of the competition also puts emphasis on quickness in using this skill as an aid to finding words in a dictionary in a minimum amount of time.

SIGHT VOCABULARY

CONCEPT: Sight Vocabulary

ACTIVITY: Word Carpet (Variation)

Several squares are drawn on the floor or pieces of paper are placed on the floor to represent Magic Carpets. Each Magic Carpet is numbered one to three to correspond with a numbered list of words on the chalkboard. The words include new vocabulary from the children's experience stories, readers, and social studies or science units. Two teams of children are selected, and each team forms a chain by holding hands. To music, the two teams walk around in circles and back and forth in a zigzag manner over the Magic Carpets until the music stops. Each child then standing on or closest to a Magic Carpet identifies any word from the numbered list on the board that corresponds with the number at that Magic Carpet. The teacher then erases that word from the list, if it is read correctly. Each team scores one point for any correctly identified word. The team with the highest score wins.

APPLICATION: This activity provides an interesting experience whereby new words are given additional emphasis. To focus on meaning of new words, the teacher can require the child who has read a word correctly to put it in a sentence in order for the team to score an additional point. Children can also be helped to identify specific word analysis clues they used to identify their words.

CONCEPT: Sight Vocabulary

ACTIVITY: Squirrel and Nut

All the children except one sit at their desks with heads resting on an arm as though sleeping but with one hand outstretched. The extra child is the Squirrel. The Squirrel who carries a nut (words on cards shaped like a nut) runs quietly about the room and drops a nut into the open hand of a child. The child jumps up from his seat, pronounces the word, and chases the Squirrel, who is safe only when he reaches his nest (seat). The activity continues with the teacher or a child selecting a new Squirrel.

APPLICATION: Words selected for the activity may come from experience stories and stories read on that or the previous day. These kinds of activities provide the necessary repetition to develop instant recognition of words and can be used to maintain words in addition to word banks and word games that the children utilize in the classroom.

COMPREHENSION

CONCEPT: Following Directions
ACTIVITY: Simon Says

The children stand about the play area facing the person who plays Simon. Every time Simon says to do something, the children must do it. However, if a command is given without the prefix "Simon says," the children must remain motionless. For example, when "Simon says take two steps," everyone must take two steps. But if Simon says, "Walk backward two steps," no one should move. If a child moves at the wrong time or turns in the wrong direction, the child puts one hand on his head. The second time he misses, he puts the other hand on his head. The third time he misses he has a point scored against him. The more quickly the commands are given and the greater number of commands, the more difficult the activity will be. The child with the lowest score wins.

APPLICATION: This activity provides children the opportunity to follow oral directions in a highly motivating situation. The rules of the activity, as adapted, allow those children who need the practice additional chances even if they have points scored against them.

CONCEPT: Following Directions
ACTIVITY: Do This, Do That

Flash cards of "Do This" and "Do That" are used in this activity. One child is selected to be the leader and stands in front of the group. The teacher holds up a flash card, and the leader makes a movement such as walking in place, running in place, swinging his arms, or hopping up and down on one foot. The children follow the actions of the leader when the sign says "Do This." When the teacher holds up the sign "Do That," the children must not move although the leader continues the action. A point is scored against a child who is caught moving. The leader can be changed frequently.

APPLICATION: This activity can be used to help children to read carefully in order to follow directions. Later, the activity can be adapted by having the leader display written directions on flash cards, for example, hop in place, jump once, walk in place, and the like.

CONCEPT: Classification

ACTIVITY: Ducks Fly

Children stand at their seats. One of them may be the leader. At the first grade level it might, in some cases, be better for the teacher to be the leader. The leader faces the class. He names different things that can fly, as ducks, birds, and airplanes. As the leader calls out "Ducks fly, Birds fly, Airplanes fly," he moves his arms as if flying. The class follows as long as he names something that can fly. If he says, "Elephants fly," and although the leader continues to keep his arms moving as if flying, the children must stop moving their arms. Those who are caught flying have a point scored against them. If the arms get tired, the leader might try things that walk, swim, and so forth, and the children then make the appropriate movement. The child with the lowest score wins.

APPLICATION: Children need to develop the skill of classifying things into groups having common characteristics. Children should be helped to note that some animals actually can do several of the movements named as flying, walking, and/or swimming. Later, children can collect pictures of animals and make a display of animals who walk, swim, and the like.

CONCEPT: Vocabulary Meaning—Colors

ACTIVITY: Rainbow

The children form a circle, facing the center. The children may be seated or standing. One child is designated the Caller and stands in the center of the circle. Instead of counting off by numbers, the children are given a small piece of paper of one of the basic colors. The Caller is given a set of word cards, one for each of the basic colors corresponding to the colors given the children in the circle. The Caller selects one word card and shows it. The children with this color attempt to change places while the Caller tries to get to one of the vacant places in the circle. The remaining child can become the new Caller or a Caller can be selected by the teacher or children. The Caller may show two word cards. Those children with the two colors then run to change places, with the Caller again trying to get to one of the vacant places in the circle. At any time, the Caller or teacher may call out "Rainbow." When this call is given, everyone must change to a different position.

APPLICATION: Children need many opportunities to develop their recognition of words in activities of this nature in which they are associating the word with the concept the word represents. This activity can be simplified in order for it to become appropriate for a language development activity. The Caller can have just color cards matching those of the children. Later, when the children have learned to match colors, the Caller can call out the names of the colors.

CONCEPT: Vocabulary Meaning—Over and Under

ACTIVITY: Over and Under Relay

The children are divided into several teams. They stand one behind the other, separated about one foot apart. A ball is given to the first person on each team, who stands at the head of the row. On a signal he passes the ball behind him over his head and calls "over." The second child in the row takes the ball and passes it between his legs and calls "under." Number three in the row takes and passes the ball over his head and calls "over" and so on down the row until the last one receives the ball. He then runs to the head of the row and starts passing the ball back in the same manner. The team whose first person reaches the head of the row first wins.

APPLICATION: This activity helps children to dramatize the meaning of the words *over* and *under*. For a variation, the teacher can hold up a card with either *over* or *under* written on it to indicate how the ball should be passed by the child moving forward to the front of the team.

CONCEPT: Vocabulary Meaning—Word Opposites

ACTIVITY: Word Change

The class is divided into two teams who line up at opposite ends of the playing area. Each child is given a word printed on a card. The words given to one team are the word opposites of the words given to the other team. One child is selected to be "It" and stands in the middle of the playing area. The teacher calls out a word, and this word and its opposite run and try to exchange places. "It" attempts to get into one of the vacated places before the two children can exchange places. The remaining child can become "It" for the next time or a new "It" can be chosen.

APPLICATION: This activity focuses on the meaning of sight vocabulary words. It can be varied with emphasis on synonyms, with teams given words that are similar in meaning.

CONCEPT: Vocabulary Meaning—Word Opposites

ACTIVITY: I'm Tall, I'm Small

The children form a circle with one child in the center. This child stands with his eyes closed. It may be helpful to have the child blindfolded.

The children in the circle walk around the circle singing or saying the following verse:

> I'm tall, I'm very small,
> I'm small, I'm very tall,
> Sometimes I'm tall,
> Sometimes I'm small,
> Guess what I am now?

As the children walk and sing "tall," "very tall," or "small," or "very small," they stretch up or stoop down, depending on the words. At the end of the singing, the teacher signals the children in the circle to assume a stretching or stooping position. The child in the center, still with eyes closed, guesses which position they have taken. For the next time another child is selected to be in the center.

APPLICATION: This movement song helps children to develop word meaning by acting out the words. Use of word opposites in this manner helps to dramatize the differences in the meaning of words. The words and actions can be changed to incorporate a larger number of "opposites", for example:

> My hands are near, my hands are far,
> Now they're far, now they're near,
> Sometimes they're near,
> Sometimes they're far,
> Guess what they are now?

The examples presented are representative of almost unlimited possibilities in structuring reading learning experiences for children. The creative teacher should be able to develop numerous activities by adapting those presented in this chapter to the developmental and skill needs of the children.

Chapter 7

ACTIVE PLAY READING CONTENT

As mentioned previously, basic facts about the nature of human beings serve educators today as principles of learning. One of these principles stated in Chapter 1 is that *learning takes place best when the child has his own purposeful goals to guide his learning activities.* This principle serves as the basis for developing active play reading content materials. Generally speaking, there are two ways in which active play reading content can be developed. These are through the *language experience stories* of children and *prepared stories.*

THE LANGUAGE EXPERIENCE STORIES OF CHILDREN

The language experience approach (LEA) can very effectively involve children developing group or individual stories based on active play experiences. This technique involves the usual procedures of the children first discussing important aspects of their experience in order for their stories to be detailed and accurate enough that other children could read their story and be able to engage in the active play situation. Such aspects of reading as sufficient detail and accuracy of information plus correct sequencing of procedures involves many higher-level cognitive aspects of problem solving.

After the discussion, the children begin to dictate their story about how to play the particular activity which the teacher records on the chalkboard or on large chart paper. It is important that the language patterns of children be recorded intact. The teacher records the words exactly as the children dictate them but spelling the words correctly. The teacher uses guided questioning to help children put in sufficient details and proper sequence in the procedure for playing the activity in the story. After the children have dictated their story, they may reread it to be sure it has enough information so that others are able to engage in the play experience after reading their story. The children may even engage in the activity again to be sure they have all the necessary steps. The language story based on such a physically oriented activity facilitates the concept that the printed word symbols represent not only their oral language but, also, these words (both oral and printed) represent things that they do, see, feel and think about.

Once the story has been developed, the teacher prepares a copy of the story on large chart paper (if the story was originally recorded on the chalkboard) and makes sufficient ditto copies for each child to keep his own copy of the story, several copies for each child (to be used later for skill development activities), and one copy for a class book of play activities, individual words, and phrases. Sentences from the stories are printed on oak tag strips.

The copy of the story on large chart paper is used for teacher-directed group or individual instruction for developing the following skills.

1. Sight vocabulary (by rereading stories; visual matching of word, phrase, sentence cards; and collecting words for children's word banks).
2. Word-attack skills and their application to context reading (by "word hunts" for words in a story that have the same word-attack pattern previously learned while working with individual words in isolation).
3. Comprehension skills of vocabulary meaning, sequence, inference, and problem solving.

The children can also help to make the class book of their active play stories by making illustrations for the book. The book can then be bound and made available for children to read on their own by putting it in the classroom or school library. Some children might even want to make up new play activities and write stories about them.

An example of such an activity by which children developed their own active play reading content stories took place in a third grade classroom. The particular reading activity was an outgrowth of a social studies unit concerned with the community and people who contribute to a community's welfare. Among the various community helpers studied, the duties of a policeman seemed to be quite fascinating. This particular class consisted largely of a low third grade group reading on first and second grade instructional level. The teacher introduced a new game about a policeman to the children and the class dictated a story about the way the new game was played. After rereading the story several times, the children played the game.

A second story was written after the children played the new game. This story was done by a remedial group of children reading on a first grade level. In a remarkably short time, each child in the group was able to read the entire story quite fluently. Reading skill activities included those mentioned above. Reading in this particular instance was fun and something in which each child could do with relatively little difficulty. It was a new experience for several in the group because reading from the basal text was difficult for them. One child reported that he "read it all for the first time." The teacher observed that this type of activity-experience story offered innumerable opportunities for a good developmental-reading lesson. She noticed that the interest appeal was high and the amount of individual success was very gratifying to each child.

PREPARED STORIES

When teachers or others prepare active play stories for children it is done on the premise of relating reading content for children to their natural urge to play. In our own work with active play stories we have found that: (1) When a child is self-motivated and interested, he reads; in this case, the reading is done without the usual motivating devices such as picture clues and illustrations; (2) active play stories are found to be extremely successful in stimulating interest in reading and at the same time improving the child's ability to read; and (3) the outcomes have been most satisfactory in terms of children's interest in reading content of this nature as well as motivation to read.

This unique kind of reading content calls for active responses to the reading task, the task being one that involves learning to play an active game, or to engage in a stunt play activity or rhythmic play activity. Such tasks bring a physical reality to printed word symbols. Over 60 such stories are presented in the final three chapters of the book. The reading levels of these stories ranges from 1.2 (2nd month of first grade) to 4.8 (8th month of fourth grade).

Active play reading content material, while enriching and extending the child's experiences, reinforces his general ability to read through his reading independently and "on his own." A child or group of children may read a story individually, in buddy teams, or as a group, with the teacher providing individual help with words when needed. After reading the story, the child or children play the game or perform the stunt or rhythmic activity. They may then reread the story and discuss how they might improve upon their first attempt at carrying out the active play task. With this procedure the child is able to develop cognitive processing skills through the physical reality of the skill involved. The child is therefore provided opportunities to practice and maintain skills necessary for meaningful reading.

A further dimension of such stories is the purpose-setting and problem-solving nature inherent in the reading activities of the stories. The child is reading to find out how to do something—play a game, or do a stunt or rhythmic activity. The child is using all his skills in reading to solve the problem of performing the task described in the story. Both purpose setting and problem solving have been identified as essential to the higher cognitive processes in mature reading. Such reading activities can provide children their first opportunities to exercise these skills with physically real experiences.

Furthermore, this approach enables the teacher to assess the child's vocabulary development and how well comprehension skills are being practiced, because the children actually demonstrate their understanding of what they read. Thus, the teacher can observe by their actions the children's comprehension. (Later in the chapter an "Inventory of Listening and/or Reading Comprehension Skills" will be provided.)

Introducing the Material

The teacher may introduce several stories by reading them to the children and then having the children play the game or demonstrate the stunt or rhythmic activity. Stories developing each type of physical activity should be selected so children will understand how the stories provide details they can use to figure out how to perform a stunt or rhythmic activity or to play a game. Sample stories should also be selected to demonstrate that some stories can be acted out by an individual child and that some require several children to participate in the activity. This latter aspect of active play reading content utilizes another basic principle stated in Chapter 1; that is, *learning takes place best when the child is given the opportunity to share cooperatively in learning experiences with his classmates under the guidance but not the control of the teacher.* As mentioned in Chapter 1, the point that should be emphasized here is that although learning may be an individual matter, it is likely to take place best in a group. This is to say that children learn individually but that socialization should be retained. Moreover, sharing in group activities seems an absolute essential in educating for democracy.

After the teacher reads a sample story, the children are asked to carry out the activity. As the children carry out the activity, the teacher *accepts* their efforts. The teacher may provide guidance *only* to the extent that is necessary to help the children identify problems and provide opportunity for them to exercise judgment in solving them and obtaining their goal: that of playing the game or performing the stunt or rhythmic activity. Parts of the story might be reread by the teacher if the children have difficulty in understanding how to carry out the activity.

Although the comprehension skills for listening and reading are the same, the sensory input is different. That is, listening is dependent upon the auditory sense, and reading is dependent upon the visual sense. The sequence of listening to reading is a natural one. However, bridging the gap to the point of handling the verbal symbols required in reading poses various problems for many children. One of the outstanding features of the approach outlined above is that the active play experience helps to serve as a bridge between listening and reading by providing direct purposeful experience for the child through active play after listening to the story.

Independent Reading and Follow-Up Play Activities

After such an introduction to the prepared stories the children should be encouraged to read them "on their own." The teacher and children might plan several procedures for using the stories. Such activities might include the following.

1. A group of children may select and read a story for a physical education class activity.
2. Individual children may select stories involving individual stunts for a physical education period.
3. After reading one of the stories an individual child may elect to act out his favorite stunt play story before a group of children. (The children might be asked to guess who or what the story describes.)
4. After reading one of the stories an individual might get several other children to read the story and participate in playing the game.

5. Children might use a buddy system for reading and acting out stories.
6. Children might write and illustrate similar-type stories for other children to read and act out.

The following are specific suggestions for procedures that might be utilized in working with the basic types of stories that appear in Chapters 8, 9, and 10.

In the first situation during which a group of children are to play a game after having read the story *Wilbur Woodchuck and His Cane,* the teacher might direct the following discussion before the children attempt to play the game.

Wilbur Woodchuck and His Cane

Wilbur Woodchuck hurt his leg.
He needed a cane.
At last his leg got better.
He did not need his cane.
He said, "I will find some friends.
We will play a game with my cane."
Wilbur's friends stood in line.
Wilbur was in front of the line.
He stood the cane in front of him.
He held it with his hand.
He called a friend's name.
Wilbur let the cane fall.
His friend caught it before it hit the ground.
He took Wilbur's place.
They played for a long time.
    Could you find something to use for a cane and play this game with other children?

TEACHER: How is Wilbur Woodchuck's game played? (Children) Do we need any specific thing in order to play this game? (Children) Good. What can we use for Wilbur's cane? (Children) That's a good idea to use a yardstick since we don't have a cane. Now, where might be a good place to mark the line? (Children) All right, Ted you may mark the line. And since you selected the story you may be the first one to be Wilbur. Where does Wilbur stand? (Children) Where do his friends stand? (Children) The rest of you may take your place along the line as Wilbur's friends. (The game is played.)

Following the activity the teacher helps the children to evaluate: What were some of the things you liked about the game? (Children) What difficulty did you have in playing the game? (Children) Yes, the yardstick did seem hard to catch when it was falling. Perhaps one of you may have a cane at home that you could loan us so we could play the game better. Some of you didn't seem to know what to do when the person does not catch the cane before it falls to the ground. What could we do to find out? (Children) Good. Let's read the story again to make sure what we are to do. (Children reread.) What does the story say to do? (Children) Then how do we know what to do? (Children) That is very good, boys and girls. Sometimes we have to "infer" from what we read. How can we help ourselves to recognize inferences? (Children) You mentioned that you enjoyed the game. Can you remember why Wilbur Woodchuck decided to make up a game? (Children) What might be another name for this game? (Children)

In a situation in which children are acting out a rhythmic play activity after reading a story, the teacher might direct the following discussion after the children have read the story "Swinging and Swaying."

Swinging and Swaying

Can you swing and sway to music?
Here are new words to "Rock-a-bye, Baby."

As you sing the words, can you think of different ways to swing and sway?

Swinging and swaying go to and fro.
Sway in the breeze turn round as you go.
Sway in the breeze turn round as you go.
Swinging and swaying go to and fro.

Could you do something different with your hands each time you sway to this song?

TEACHER: You've selected an interesting story for us today, Mary and Susan. Can you tell us why you chose this one for everyone to read? (Children) Yes, I'm sure most everyone does know the song "Rock-a-bye, Baby." I have it here, let's listen to it (Children listen). In our story something about our song has been changed. Can anyone tell me what it is? (Children) What did you think was swinging and swaying in the new words? (Children) You have some good ideas. Let's all swing and sway now as we hear the music. Try to sing along with the new words.

(Children) That's a good idea. Let's sing the new words together. (Children) Fine. Are we ready to sing now? (Children) Yes, it is hard not to forget to sing the new words. You did very well. Now, let's swing and sway as we sing. Are we all going to do the same thing? (Children) Good. I'll be interested in seeing how each of you swings and sways in the breeze. (Children sing and demonstrate rhythmic activity.) Very good, boys and girls. How many said they were flowers? (Children) How many of you were trees? (Children) And Johnny, you said you were tall grass in the fields. I could almost see tall grass by the way you were swaying and turning around. What were some of the different things you all did with your hands each time you swayed to this song? (Children demonstrate.) All right. Let's try it again. (Children sing and demonstrate.) I can see some of you were gentle breezes and some of you were almost like a "high wind" in a storm. Who can tell which of you were more like "high wind?" (Children) What did they do to be like a "high wind?" (Children) They must really have liked this song. Perhaps we could make up a story about all kinds of winds someday soon.

In a situation during which children are taking turns acting out their favorite stunt play story the teacher might direct the following discussion after a child's presentation of *George Giraffe*.

George Giraffe

> There is a tall animal in a faraway land.
> He has a long neck.
> His name is George Giraffe.
> You could look like him if you did this.
> Place your arms high over your head.
> Put your hands together.
> Point them to the front.
> This will be his neck and head.
> Now walk like George Giraffe.
> This is how.
> Stand on your toes.
> Walk with your legs straight.
> Could you walk so you would look like George Giraffe?

TEACHER: Wasn't that interesting the way Becky showed us how George Giraffe looked? (Children) What do you think George Giraffe looked like from what Becky did? (Children) What did Becky do to look like George Giraffe? What did Becky do to have a long neck like George Giraffe?

(Children) Can someone else make a long neck? (Children demonstrate.) Oh, you are *all* very good at making long necks. Particularly Jimmy. How did Becky walk to be like George Giraffe? Can someone show us: (Children demonstrate.) What do you have to do to walk like George Giraffe? (Children) Is it easy to pretend to be a giraffe? Let's try it and find out. (All children demonstrate.) Did you feel awkward? (Children) We often say the giraffes look "ungainly" or "awkward." Do you think these are good words to describe a giraffe? (Children) Can you think of other words we might use to describe a giraffe? (Children) Can you think of other animals that also look "ungainly" or "awkward?" (Children) That was good, Becky. You really showed us how to look like a giraffe. You must have read the story very carefully. Bobby, you said you also had read the story about George Giraffe. Why do I say "Becky must have read very carefully?" (Bobby) That's right. It is important to use all the information the story gives to help you pretend to be something. That was fun, wasn't it? (Children) All right. Now Mary is going to tell us about her story. But this time we are going to do it differently. This time Mary is *not* going to tell us the name of her story, or what she is pretending to be. We will have to guess *who* or *what* she is. (In this manner the group continues to share, discuss, act out and evaluate the stories the children present.)

This approach enables the teacher to assess the child's vocabulary development and how well comprehension skills are being practiced, because the children actually demonstrate their understanding of what they listen to or what they read. The following evaluation form can be used for that purpose.

INVENTORY OF LISTENING
and/or READING COMPREHENSION SKILLS
Group or Individual

Directions: Check YES or NO to indicate proficiency or lack of proficiency with which children are using skills.

SKILLS

YES NO

___ ___ 1. Getting Facts
           Do children understand what to do and how to do it?

___ ___ 2. Selecting Main Idea
           Do children use succinct instructions in preparing
           for and playing the activity?

YES   NO

_____ _____   3. Organizing Main Ideas by Enumeration and
                   Sequence
                   Do children know the number of participants
                   needed and the order in which the activity is
                   performed?

_____ _____   4. Following Directions
                   Do children proceed with the activity according to
                   the precise instructions in the story?

_____ _____   5. Drawing Inference
                   Do children seem to draw reasonable conclusions as
                   shown by the way they imitate the animal, person, or
                   object in the story?

_____ _____   6. Gaining Independence in Word Mastery
                   Do children use phonetic and structural analysis to
                   get a word without asking for help?

_____ _____   7. Building Meaningful Vocabulary
                   Do children use the words in the story (circle, leader,
                   line and so on) in their speaking vocabulary as they
                   organize and play the activity?

_____ _____   8. Distinguishing Fact from Fantasy
                   Do children indicate which stories are real and
                   which are imaginary?

Guidelines for Developing Prepared Stories

Active play stories can be developed by the teacher or others. This has been successfully done by some teachers who have produced very creative stories using games, rhythmic play activities and stunt play activities. Teachers have also involved children in such projects as creative writing experiences. In writing such stories using an active play setting there are several guidelines that one should keep in mind.

In general, the new word load should be kept relatively low. There should be as much repetition of these words as seems appropriate. Sentence length and lack of complexity in sentences should be considered in keeping the level of difficulty of material within the independent reading levels of children. If desired, there are numerous readability formulas that can be utilized. However, we hasten to mention that one should not necessarily rely on such formulas. For example, The Michigan Reading Association in describing *readability* asserts that the ease with which a person can read printed materials, called readability, is related to many factors. These factors are *not* measured by conventional readability formulas which are based on length of sentences and the number of long or multisyllabic words.

Consideration must also be given to the reading values and literary merits of the story. Using a character or characters in a story setting helps to develop interest. If a game is to be used in the story it should not be readily identifiable. For example, the game "Catch the Cane" is not immediately evident in the story, "Wilbur Woodchuck and His Cane." When children identify an activity early in a story, there can be resulting minimum attention on the part of the readers to get the necessary details in order to play the activity. In developing an active play story, therefore, it is important that the nature of the activity and procedures of it unfold gradually.

In developing an active play story the equipment, playing area, and procedures should be clearly described. Correct terminology should be used in describing the setting. In a *file, row,* or *column* the children stand one behind the other. In a *line* the children stand beside each other. Basic motor skills that can be utilized in stunt and rhythmic activities as well as for games include *locomotor skills* (walking, running, leaping, jumping, hopping, skipping and galloping and sliding); *throwing* and *striking skills* (and rolling) with underarm, sidearm, and overarm swing patterns; *catching* and *axial movements* (twisting, turning, and stretching).

In summary, active play reading content provides variety to the reading program. High interest and motivation are the results of purposeful reading and bringing words into physical reality by playing a game, performing a stunt, or responding to a rhythm.

Chapter 8

ACTIVE GAME READING CONTENT

For purposes of discussion here, we will consider games as *active interactions of children in competitive and/or cooperative situations*. This description of games places emphasis on *active* games as opposed to those that are *passive* in nature. This is to say that active games are concerned with a total or near total physical response of children as they interact with each other.

Games play a very important part in our society. The unique quality of games and their application to situations in everyday living have become a part of various colloquial expressions. In many instances, descriptive word phrases from games have become part of daily vocabulary and appear frequently in news articles and other written material. These words and phrases are used to describe a situation that is so familiar in a game situation that they give a clear meaning to an event from real life.

Many of us have used, at one time or another, the expression "that's the way the ball bounces" to refer to a situation in which the outcome was not as desirable as was anticipated. Or, "that's par for the course," meaning that the difficulty was anticipated and the results were no better or no worse than expected. When we are "home free" we tend to refer to having gotten out of a tight situation, with results better than expected. The expression "the bases are loaded" describes a situation in which a critical point has been reached and there is much at stake on the next event or series of events. If you have "two strikes against you," you are operating at a grave disadvantage, and if someone "strikes out," he has failed.

It is interesting to consider how the game preferences of a particular country give insight into their culture, and this has been an important area of study and research by sociologists in recent years. The national games, the popular games, and the historical games in which the people of a nation engage provide insight into their culture. They are as much a cultural expression as their books, theater, and art.

The value of games as an important intellectual influence in the school program has been recognized for decades. For example, as far back as 1909, Bancroft[1] observed that as a child's perceptions are quickened, he sees more quickly that the ball is coming toward him, that he is in danger of being tagged, or that it is his turn; he hears footsteps behind him, or his name or number called; he feels the touch on the shoulder; or, in innumerable other ways, he is aroused to quick and direct recognition of, and response to, things that go on around him.

The physiological value of games has often been extolled because of the vigorous physical nature of many game activities in which children participate. And in more recent years a great deal of credence has been put in the potentialities for modifying human behavior within a social frame of reference which many games tend to provide. For instance, it is possible that the game is probably the child's first social relationship with strangers and his first testing of self against others.

COMPETITION AND COOPERATION IN GAMES

It should be recalled that our description of active games previously given took into account both cooperative and competitive situations. In view of the fact that there has been a considerable amount of interest in competitive activities for children, it seems appropriate that we discuss this, particularly as it relates to games.

It is interesting to note that the terms *cooperation* and *competition* are antonymous; therefore, the reconciliation of children's competitive needs and cooperative needs is not an easy matter. In a sense we are confronted with an ambivalent condition which, if not carefully handled, could place children in a state of conflict. This was recognized over half a century ago when Horney[2] recognized that on the one hand everything is done to spur us toward success, which means that we must not only be assertive but aggressive, able to push others out of the way. On the other hand, we are deeply imbued with ideals which declare that it is selfish to want anything for ourselves, that we should be humble, turn the other hand, be yielding. Thus, modern society not only rewards one kind of behavior (cooperation) but its direct opposite (competition). Perhaps more often than not our cultural demands sanction these rewards with-

---

1. Bancroft, Jessie H. *Games* (New York, The Macmillan Company, 1909).

2. Horney, Karen, *The Neurotic Personality of Our Times* (New York, W. W. Norton & Company, Inc., 1937).

out provision of clear-cut standards of value with regard to specific conditions under which these forms of behavior might well be practiced. Hence, the child is placed in somewhat of a quandary as to when to compete and when to cooperate.

More recently, it has been found that competition does not necessarily lead to peak performance and may in fact interfere with achievement. In this connection, Kohn[3] reported on a survey on the effects of competition on sports, business, and classroom achievement and found that 65 studies showed that cooperation promoted higher achievement than competition, eight showed the reverse and 36 showed no statistically significant difference. It was concluded that the trouble with competition is that it makes one person's success depend upon another's failure, and as a result when success depends on sharing resources, competition can get in the way.

In generalizing on the basis of available evidence with regard to the subject of competition, it seems justifiable to formulate the following concepts:

1. Very young children in general are not very competitive but become more so as they grow older.
2. There is a wide variety in competition among children; that is, some are violently competitive, while others are mildly competitive, and still others are not competitive at all.
3. Boys tend to be more competitive than girls.
4. Competition should be adjusted so that there is not a preponderant number of winners over losers.
5. Competition and rivalry produce results in effort and speed of accomplishment.

In any teaching-learning situation one might well be guided by the above concepts. As far as active games are concerned, they are not only a good medium for the various aspects of growth and development of children, but, under the guidance of skillful teachers, they can also provide for competitive needs of children in a pleasurable and enjoyable way.

---

3. Kohn, A., *No Contest: The Case Against Competition* (Boston. Houghton-Mifflin Co.). 1986.

ORGANIZATION OF GAME ACTIVITIES

The benefits that can be derived from participation in game activities are more likely to accrue when these activities are properly organized. The following discussions will focus upon general organization, signaling and organization of classroom games.

General Organization

Many games begin from certain standard formations which include circles and lines. In a *circle* formation children ordinarily stand facing inward toward the center. The leader (teacher) should be a part of the circle rather than in the center of it so as to be able to see and be seen by all children. Forming a circle of young children for the first time can be done by the leader taking the hand of one child and then each child in turn taking the hand of another. The leader "circles around" and takes the hand of the last child to form the circle. After the children understand the concept of a circle the leader can ordinarily just simply tell them to arrange themselves in a circle. Circles may be made larger by each child taking a specified number of steps backward, and smaller by taking steps forward.

In some cases games played from a circle formation have been much maligned on the basis that there is too much inactivity of children just standing in a circle. It is doubtful if such criticism is entirely justified, because the skillful leader can conduct this type of activity in such a way that there will be equal opportunity for participation. Leaders should guard against having a circle too large in those kinds of games that involve only two children as principal performers at one time. Small circles afford many more turns.

Some feel that the circle formation has a positive psychological effect, in that it tends to provide a spirit of unity among the participants. That is, each player can see and become aware of the performance of other players in the group.

It is interesting to note that holding hands in a circle game has important connotations for social interaction through *tactile communication*. Some writers have called attention to the possibilities of this by suggesting that better human relations can be obtained through intrinsic tactile communication in the utilization of activities requiring *touch*. In fact, some studies have shown that such tactile communication provides a basis for the attraction that is necessary for black and white children to form positive relationships. More specifically, it has been found that recorded incidents of tactile interaction between black and white children are equivalent to the recorded incidents of tactile interaction between black children and black children and those between white children and white children.

In a *line* formation the children stand side by side to form the line. When they have learned the idea of a line the leader can get them into this formation by merely telling them to make as many lines as are needed after the class has been divided into the appropriate number of groups for a given activity.

In any kind of formation the leader should be alert to a lack of interest on the part of the participants. This is usually observed when some children are not afforded the opportunity to participate because of too large a number of players. This situation can be avoided to a certain extent by such practices as having several runners and/or chasers rather than just one, and putting more than one ball into play when practical where directions for play call for only one ball.

Signaling

As in any kind of human endeavor, every game has a beginning and an ending. All games begin with some sort of signal, but there are different ways in which a game can end. For example, a game can be played for a specified amount of time or it can continue until a particular objective has been accomplished. In some instances it may be necessary to stop a game before its completion and this requires some sort of signal.

Generally speaking, signals used for games can be broadly classified as *natural* signals and *mechanical* signals. An example of a natural starting signal would be in a game such as "Hill Dill." The signal to start the game is "Hill Dill run over the hill." The first few words tend to get the attention of the players and the last word "hill" starts the game.

If a game does not have a particular statement or saying to get it started, the leader or a child can get it started by simply saying, "Ready! Go!" The word "ready" gets the attention and the word "go" starts the game.

Mechanical signals require some sort of device and can be further classified into *sight* and *sound* signals. An example of a sight signal is the use of a flag or piece of cloth. Sometimes such sight-signaling devices can be of different colors and waved in different ways so as to have specific meaning for children.

The most common of the sounding devices is a whistle, although signaling with a horn or a bell can also be used. Ordinarily, the use of mechanical signals can be kept to a minimum for starting and stopping games. If a sounding device such as a whistle is used at all, it is perhaps best to use it only for stopping activities. Children then become accustomed to associating the sound of the whistle with *stopping* activity. If a whistle is used to both start and stop games, confusion can sometimes result.

Organization for Classroom Games

On occasion, it is necessary to confine game activities to the limited area of the regular classroom when no other space is available. At first glance this might appear impossible. Nevertheless, with wise planning and effective organization it is possible to conduct certain games' activities within the limited confines of the average classroom. Although chasing and fleeing games may not be adaptable to the classroom, games of circle formation, stationary relays, and other games that require little space afford much enjoyment for children.

The following discussion of organization for participation in classroom games need not be thought of only in terms of game activities. This is to say that the suggestions that follow can also apply to rhythmic play activities (Chapter 9) and stunt play activities (Chapter 10) in the classroom situation. With this general idea in mind, the following discussion will focus upon ways to prepare the classroom for activities.

The way in which one organizes for classroom activities will depend generally upon such factors as the kinds of activities to be taught and time required to arrange the room before and after activity. The following suggestions for preparing the classroom for activity have certain advantages and disadvantages, and for this reason the above factors need to be taken into account. In all of the following plans it is expected that a system will be devised whereby the children will be able to prepare the room effectively and efficiently under the guidance of the teacher.

1. *Clear the room of all furniture.* The obvious advantage of this plan is that a maximum amount of space is provided for activity. However,

an inordinate amount of time may be required to get the furniture in and out of the room. In addition, furniture in the hall outside the room can possibly cause an obstruction.

2. *Move furniture to one side.* This procedure will provide a little more than half of the room for activity. It has the advantage of not being time consuming for room preparation.

3. *Place furniture on all sides around the walls.* With this plan all space is available for use, with the exception of three or four feet taken up by the furniture around the walls. An advantage of this plan is that children who are not participating due to lack of space are in a good position to observe those who are participating. With this arrangement, however, it is not always as easy to get the furniture back to its original position as quickly as when furniture is placed at the side of the room. In this regard some plan of organization should be effected, regardless of how the room is prepared, to get children in and out of activities with little loss of time.

4. *Place furniture in center of room.* This plan is useful when circle games are to be used if there is no need to have performers within the circle. The circle is arranged around the furniture and thus is not an encumbrance. This arrangement also provides for the possibility of having children in as many as four small groups in each corner of the room. This is particularly useful for individual activities, such as stunt play activities.

5. *Leave the room as it is.* This, of course, depends upon the original arrangement of the furniture. For example, if it is arranged in rows, relays can be conducted using the aisles between the rows as paths to run the relays.

GENERAL TEACHING PROCEDURES FOR GAMES

By and large it seems advisable that games be presented in terms of the whole activity. Thus, the child should gain an insight into the requirements necessary for successful performance in the game. As a result, he or she should develop an appreciation of the skills involved in playing the game to the best of his or her ability. In games of low organization that have a few simple rules and involve little strategy, this procedure may be carried out with little or no difficulty. As games become more complex, however, part-whole relationships need to be made meaningful to children. This means that leaders should take into account the important factor of like elements appearing in various games. For example, running is an element common to many different kinds of games. As games become more complex, more elements may be added or methods of performing the various elements may become more complex. In presenting games to children at the various age levels, it becomes necessary that the leader understand that a single presentation may be a part related to other parts within a whole. This implies that leaders must analyze games for the purpose of providing those that reflect the growth and development of the child in relation to the gradated complexity of the games. The following additional guides are recommended as a help in the successful presentation of game activities to children.

1. Be sure all necessary equipment is readily accessible. It may be a good idea to conceal equipment until proper time for use. A ball can sometimes become an attention-distracting factor. (A small bag is useful in concealing equipment.)
2. A game may be related to something that children already know about. If it resembles another game they have played, this should be indicated. Aspects of the game can be related to another subject-matter area, thus providing an outstanding opportunity for the cognitive aspect of active play.
3. Determine the best formation for arrangement of the children when the game is being explained or demonstrated. In some cases it may be best to have the children in the regular game formation when presenting it. This may be an advantage if the formation is compact or if there is a small number of children.
4. Use diagrams and visual aids when necessary. This procedure may be useful when the teacher is explaining the game in the classroom before going on to the outdoor activity area.
5. Start the game as soon as is feasibly possible. The game should not be stopped too often to make corrections; however, spot evaluation may take place as seems necessary.
6. Strive for maximum activity for all children by utilizing such procedures as two circles instead of one for a large group in a circle game. Avoid game procedures which tend to eliminate players.
7. Be alert to all safety hazards involved in the game. For example, in a game where children run for a goal, the goal line should be a reasonably safe distance from the wall rather than the wall itself used as the goal.

ACTIVE GAME STORIES

Roy Rabbit and His Friends

Roy Rabbit has a ball.
He stands with many friends.
They stand close together.
Roy drops the ball.
The friends run.
He calls a friend's name.
That friend must get the ball.
He gets it.
He calls, "Stand."
All friends stop.
He rolls the ball at a friend.
This friend is "It."
They play again.
   Could you play this game the same way as Roy Rabbit and his friends?

Do What Jack Does

Can you do what Jack does?
In this game the children stand behind one another.
One child is Jack.
He is first.
Jack walks.
He jumps.
He hops.
He skips.
He runs.
The other children try to do everything Jack does.
It is fun to follow Jack.
How can he go so fast?
How can he do so many things?
Jack walks like a bear.
Sally misses.
Jack jumps like a rabbit.
Dick misses.
Jane is the last one to miss.
She is the Jack for the next game.
   How long could you do what Jack does?

Sparky Sparrow Plays A Game

The birds are asleep in their nests.
Sparky Sparrow does not have a nest.
He says, "I will have some fun."
He calls, "Fly!"
The birds find other nests.
They have fun.
Could you show other children how to play Sparky Sparrow's game?

The Little Bees Have Fun

One day some bees got together.
They wanted to play a game.
They talked to each other.
One bee said, "Let each of us find a friend."
Each bee found a friend.
Each bee faced his friend.
One bee stood alone.
His name was Busy Bee.
He was "It."
Busy Bee said, "Buzz."
All bees found another friend.
Busy Bee tried to find a friend.
One bee did not find a friend.
Now he was Busy Bee.
They played and played.
Could you play this game like the bees?

Throw The Ball

Do you like to play with a ball?
Here is a game you can play.
Children are in a ring.
One child is in the center of the ring.
He has a ball.
He throws the ball into the air.
He calls a child's name.
That child tries to catch the ball.
Another child throws the ball into the air.
He calls a name.
The game goes on and on.
Will you try to play this game with others?

Oswald Octopus and His Friends

Oswald Octopus lives in the sea.
He has a big head.
He has big eyes.
He has many long arms.
Oswald Octopus plays a game with the fish.
The fish go to one side.
Oswald Octopus says, "All fish swim."
The fish try to get to the other side.
Oswald Octopus tries to catch them.
When a fish is caught, he helps Oswald.
They play until all fish are caught.
Then they play the game again.

Could you and other children play this game the way Oswald Octopus played it with his fish friends?

Wilbur Woodchuck and His Cane

Wilbur Woodchuck hurt his leg.
He needed a cane.
At last his leg got better.
He did not need his cane.
He said, "I will find some friends. We will play a game with my cane."
Wilbur's friends stood in line.
Wilbur was in front of the line.
He stood the cane in front of him.
He held it with his hand.
He called a friend's name.
Wilbur let the cane fall.
His friend caught it before it hit the ground.
He took Wilbur's place.
They played for a long time.

Could you find something to use for a cane and play this game with other children?

Billy Bear in the Circle

Once upon a time many bears played in the big woods.
The bears stood in a circle.
Billy Bear stood inside the circle.
Billy Bear was "It."
The other bears held paws to make a circle.
Then Billy Bear tried to get out.

He tried to go under to get out.
The other bears tried to keep Billy Bear in the circle.
At last Billy Bear got out.
He ran fast.
All the bears ran after Billy Bear.
One of the bears caught Billy Bear.
That bear was "It" for the next game.
Now he was Billy Bear.
Could you play this game with other children?

Freddy Fox and His Friends

Freddy Fox met his friends.
He wanted to play with them.
He said, "I know a game. This is how to play. All stand in a circle. I will be 'It.' I will be in the center. I will call two names. Those two try to change places. If I call 'dog' and 'cat' they try to change. I will try to get a place. If I get a place the one left is 'It.' Try not to be 'It.' Are you ready? Let's try the game."
Could you and your friends have animal names and play the game like Freddy Fox and his friends?

The Indian Game

Do you know any Indian games?
I know one.
It is fun.
This is how the Indians play it.
All but one of the Indians stand close together in a circle.
They stand so close they touch each other.
One Indian stands outside the circle.
He walks around the circle.
He taps a friend and says, "Come with me."
His friend follows him around the circle.
He taps another friend and says, "Come with me."
His friends follow him around the circle.
He taps another friend and says, "Come with me."
This friend follows along.
He taps many friends.
Each time he says, "Come with me."
They all follow around the circle.
At last the first Indian shouts, "Go home!"
All try to get to their places.
The first Indian tries to get a place.

One is left out.
He starts the next game.
   Could you play this Indian game with your friends?

Barney Bear Watches the Squirrels

One day Barney Bear went for a walk
He walked until he came to a hill.
He sat down to rest.
All at once he heard a noise.
He got up and walked to the top of the hill.
On the other side he saw many squirrels.
He said to himself, "I will watch them. They seem to be having fun."
He saw that each squirrel stood with a partner.
Each squirrel held his partner's paw.
He saw two squirrels who did not stand together.
He watched these two.
He saw one start to chase the other.
The squirrel being chased linked arms with another squirrel.
This made three squirrels.
Then one had to leave.
He was being chased.
He linked arms with another squirrel.
Then this squirrel's partner was caught.
Then they played again.
Barney Bear thought this game was fun.
He went home and showed his bear friends the game.
   Could you show other children how to play this game?

Sammy Squirrel

One day Sammy Squirrel met some friends.
They wanted to run and play.
Sammy's friends went to one end of the field.
Sammy stayed in the center of the field.
He was "It."
When Sammy said, "Change," his friends ran to the other end.
Sammy tried to tag them.
He tagged one.
Now he was Sammy's helper.
Sammy said, "Change," again.
The squirrels ran back to the other end.
More squirrels were tagged.

They were Sammy's helpers.
Each time Sammy said, "Change," they ran to the other end.
They played until only one squirrel was left.
He was "It" for the next game.
    Could you play this game with your friends?

The Dodging Bear

One day some bears met in the woods.
Teddy Bear had found a ball.
The other bears wanted to play with the ball.
They thought of a game to play.
Teddy Bear said, "Everyone hold paws and make a circle."
Teddy Bear went to the center of the circle.
He gave the ball to Tommy Bear.
Tommy Bear threw the ball at Teddy Bear.
Teddy Bear dodged.
Then Timmy Bear threw the ball at Teddy Bear.
Teddy Bear dodged again.
Other bears tried to hit Teddy Bear with the ball.
At last he was hit with the ball by one of the bears.
This bear's name was Tony Bear.
Teddy Bear changed places with Tony Bear.
Now the bears tried to hit Tony Bear with the ball.
Soon Tony Bear was hit.
He changed places with the bear who hit him with the ball.
They played and played.
    Could you get a rubber ball and play this game with other children?

The Train Game

Let's make a train.
Do you know how?
Three children stand one behind the other.
They hold on to the waist of the child in front of them.
The first child is the engine.
The second child is the passenger car.
The last car is called the "caboose."
Make many trains.
Have three children for each train.
Now we can play a train game.
Have one child be "It."
He tries to hook on to one of the trains.

He does this by putting his hands on the waist of the caboose.
When he does, the "engine" of the train becomes "It."
Try to play the train game.
 Could you and some of your friends become trains and play the train game?

The Wolves and the Sheep

Three wolves are asleep in their den.
On the other side of the field there are many sheep.
The sheep go near the wolves' den.
The sheep who is the leader says, "Who lives there?"
The leader of the wolves says, "Cows live here."
The sheep do not run.
The leader of the wolves says, "Dogs live here."
The sheep do not run.
The leader of the wolves says, "Wolves live here."
The sheep run back to their end of the field.
The wolves try to catch them before the sheep get back.
All the sheep who were caught are put in the wolves' den.
The sheep who were not caught come again to the wolves' den.
They do the same as before.
The last three sheep caught become the wolves.
They start all over again.
 Could you play this game with some of your friends?

The Chasing Game

Let's play a chasing game.
Children stand in a ring.
One child is in the center of the ring.
He closes his eyes.
He turns around and around.
He stops and points to a child.
This child runs.
All children chase him.
One child taps him.
He is "It" for the next game.
 Could you play this game at school and at home?

The Kittens and the Ball of Yarn

Have you ever heard of kittens playing with a ball of yarn?
They do many things with it.
Once some kittens found a ball of yarn.

This is what they did.
They stood close together in a circle.
The kittens in the circle passed the ball of yarn around.
Each kitten would take it.
He would try to pass it to the next kitten.
They tried to pass it quickly.
Do you know what the kitten outside the circle tried to do?
He ran around outside the circle.
He tried to tag the ball of yarn.
Once he did tag it.
Then he changed places with the kitten who had it.
They had fun with this game.
They played for a long time.
    Could you use a rubber ball instead of a ball of yarn and play this game with other children?

The Shadow Game

Have you ever watched shadows?
When do you see your shadow?
What can your shadow do?
Here is a game to play with shadows.
You can play it with one or more children.
You can be "It."
Tell your friends to run around so you cannot step on their shadow.
When you step on a shadow, that child becomes "It."
You join the other players.
    Could you step on someone's shadow?

The Bird Game

Some birds play games.
You can play a bird game with friends.
Many children can play.
Have the children play they are birds.
Some children can be redbirds.
Some children can be bluebirds.
Some children can be blackbirds.
Some children can be yellow birds.
All the children get together.
They choose a child for a Bird Catcher.
Bird Catcher calls, "Redbirds."
All redbirds run.
Bird Catcher tries to catch them.

Bird Catcher calls other birds.
He tries to tag the other birds.
They play until all are tagged.
They choose another Bird Catcher.
They play again.
    Could you play the bird game with other children?

Poochie Poodle and Clarabelle Cat

Poochie Poodle is a brave little dog.
He enjoys scampering around and chasing other animals.
One animal he likes to chase most is Clarabelle Cat.
One day he was chasing Clarabelle Cat all around the lawn.
Some children saw Poochie chasing Clarabelle.
They wanted to help Clarabelle.
They stood in a circle and held hands.
Clarabelle Cat went in the center of the circle.
Poochie Poodle stayed outside the circle.
Poochie tried to get in the circle to catch Clarabelle.
The children tried to keep him out.
Soon Poochie got inside the circle.
Then the children let Clarabelle get out of the circle.
It was like a game.
Finally, Poochie caught Clarabelle.
Then they both stood in the circle with the children.
One of the children said, "I will be Poochie Poodle."
Another child said, "I will be Clarabelle Cat."
They played the game again and again.
    Would you like to choose one child to be Poochie Poodle and one
child to be Clarabelle Cat and play the game?

Traffic Lights

Traffic lights help us to travel safely.
The green light means "Go."
The yellow light means "Come to a stop."
The red light means "Stop."
This game is called Traffic Lights.
It is a good running game.
Here is one way to play it.
There are two lines.
One is the starting line.
The other is the goal line.
One player is "It."

The other players stand behind the starting line.

The player who is "It" has his back to the other players.

The player who is "It" closes his eyes and he says, "One, two, three, green light, one, two, three yellow light."

The other players run quickly and quietly toward the goal line.

Then the player who is "It" says, "One, two, three, red light."

He opens his eyes and turns around quickly.

The other players try to stop.

If "It" sees any children moving, he sends them back to the starting line to start over again.

All the children try to get to the goal line.

The one who gets there first wins.

He is "It" for the next game.

Could you and your friends play Traffic Lights together?

Chippy Chipmunk and His Friends

One day Chippy Chipmunk met some chipmunk friends.

They stood around and talked.

After a time all except two of them stood together in a circle.

Chippy Chipmunk and Charlie Chipmunk went outside the circle.

Chippy Chipmunk began to chase Charlie.

Charlie stood in front of Chester Chipmunk.

Now Charlie chased Chester.

He tagged him before Chester stood in front of another chipmunk.

Chester then became the chaser.

Charlie became the runner.

This was because he had been tagged by Chester.

The chipmunks played until all had a chance to be a chaser and a runner.

Could you make a circle with some other children and play the game the way the chipmunks played it?

The Chasing Dogs

Did you know that some dogs learn to do tricks?

One thing they can learn to do is "fetch."

The dog's master throws out something and says, "Fetch."

With much practice the dog can learn to bring it back to his master.

There is a game about dogs chasing a ball.

The game is called "Dog Chase."

This is the way to play it.

The children go into five or six groups.

Each group takes the name of a dog.

One group can be poodles.

Another group can be terriers and so on until all groups have a dog name.

Now all small groups make one large group.

One child is the master.

The master throws a rubber ball away from the group.

The master calls a dog name.

All of the children in the group with this dog name chase after the ball.

The child who gets the ball first becomes the master for the next game.

Could you get a rubber ball and play "Dog Chase" with some other children?

The Monkeys and the Coconut

One day some monkeys met in the jungle.

One monkey climbed a tree.

He picked a coconut from the tree.

Mickey Monkey said, "Let's play a game with the coconut."

"I will tell you how. All stand in a circle. Put your feet apart. Your feet should touch the feet next to you. I will stand in the center of the circle. I will roll the coconut. I will try to roll it between someone's legs. If I do, that one will change places with me. Then he will be in the circle. When the coconut goes between someone's legs it will count one point against him. When we finish, the one who has the lowest number of points will be the winner. Let's play the game."

Could you get a rubber ball and play this game with friends?

Tommy's Dream

One night Tommy had a dream.

He dreamed he saw some children playing a game.

Some of the children formed a circle.

Other children were in the center of the circle.

The children who formed the circle had a large rubber ball.

They tried to hit the children inside the circle with the ball.

They tried to hit below the waist.

They did this so the children inside the circle would not get hurt.

A child inside the circle was hit with the ball.

He changed places with the child who hit him.

They played and played.

Each time a child was hit he changed places with the child who hit him.

Tommy woke in the morning.

He remembered his dream.

He decided that when he went to school that day he would make his dream come true.

If you were Tommy, how would you make the dream come true?

Chapter 9

RHYTHMIC PLAY READING CONTENT

The term "rhythm" is derived from the Greek word *rhythmos*, which means "measured motion." One of the most desirable media for child expression through movement is found in rhythmic activities. One need look only to the functions of the human body to see the importance of rhythm in the life of the child. The heart beats in rhythm, the digestive processes function in rhythm, breathing is done in rhythm; in fact, almost anything in which human beings are involved is done in a more or less rhythmic pattern.

CLASSIFICATION OF RHYTHMIC PLAY ACTIVITIES

One approach to the classification of rhythmic play activities centers around the kinds of rhythmic experiences that one might wish children to have. It is recommended here that these experiences consist of (1) unstructured experiences, (2) semistructured experiences, and (3) structured experiences. It should be understood that in this particular way of grouping rhythmic experiences a certain amount of overlapping will occur as far as the degree of structuring is concerned. That is, although an experience is classified as an unstructured one, there could possibly be some small degree of structuring in certain kinds of situations. With this idea in mind the following descriptions of these three types of rhythmic experiences are submitted.

Unstructured experiences include those in which there is an original or creative response and in which there has been little, if any, previous explanation or discussion in the form of specific directions. The *semistructured* experiences include those in which certain movements or interpretations are suggested by the teacher, a child, or a group of children. *Structured* experiences involve the more difficult rhythmic patterns associated with various types of dances. A well-balanced program of rhythmic play activities should provide opportunities for these various types of rhythmic experiences.

134

ACCOMPANIMENT FOR RHYTHMIC ACTIVITIES

There are many different forms of accompaniment that are suitable for use with rhythmic play activities. All of these can be useful when employed under the right conditions. At the same time all of them have certain disadvantages. In the final analysis it will be up to the teacher to select the form of accompaniment that will best meet the needs in a particular situation.

Five forms of accompaniment for rhythmic play activities are presented here along with what might be considered as advantages and disadvantages of each.

1. *Clapping* as a form of accompaniment can be useful in helping children gain a better understanding of tempo. There is also something to be said for the child actually becoming a part of the accompaniment on a physical basis, since it gives him a feeling that he is more involved. This is particularly important in the early stages when rhythmic activities are being introduced. Clapping can be done with the hands or by slapping various parts of the body such as the thighs or knees. A major disadvantage of clapping as a form of accompaniment is that it is virtually impossible to obtain a melody through this procedure.

2. Various kinds of percussion instruments may be used as accompaniment, the most prominent being the *drum*. The drum is an instrument which is easy to learn to play and the person furnishing the accompaniment can change the tempo as he or she wishes. Actually, some kinds of dances such as some of the Indian dances require the use of a drum as accompaniment. Likewise, as in the case of clapping, the use of a drum makes it difficult to have a melody with the accompaniment.

3. *Singing* as a form of accompaniment is ordinarily required in movement songs and in square dances where singing calls are used. All children can become involved as in the case of clapping. One of the disadvantages of singing as a form of accompaniment is that the singing voices may become weaker as the child participates in the activity. For example, if a movement song requires a great deal of skipping, it is difficult for the child to do both tasks of singing and skipping for a very long period of time.

4. At one time the *piano* was a very popular form of accompaniment for rhythmic play activities. The chief disadvantage of the piano is

that it is a difficult instrument to learn to play and all teachers have not included it as a part of their professional preparation. Another disadvantage is that even though one is an accomplished pianist, the player must obviously be at the piano and thus is away from the activity. The piano has an advantage, in that a melody can be obtained with it.

5. Perhaps the most popular form of accompaniment at the present time is *recordings*. Sources of this form of accompaniment are so plentiful that almost any kind of accompaniment is available. One of the distinct disadvantages of recordings concerns those that furnish instructions intended for children. Sometimes these instructions are confusing and too difficult for younger children to understand. The teacher should evaluate such instructions and determine if the above is the case. If it is found that the instructions are too difficult for a particular group of children, the teacher can use just the musical accompaniment. The major advantage of recordings is that they are professionally prepared. However, teachers might well consider using a tape recorder to record their own music or singing voices of children as forms of accompaniment.

(The rhythmic play stories presented later in the chapter are concerned with three categories: *creative rhythms, movement songs,* and *dances.*)

CREATIVE RHYTHMS

Creative experience involves *self*-expression. It is concerned with the need to experiment, to express original ideas, to think, to react. Creativity and childhood enjoy a congruous relationship, in that children are naturally creative. They imagine. The pretend. They are unhibited. They are not only original but actually ingenious in their thoughts and actions. Indeed, creativity is a characteristic inherent in the lives of practically all children. It may range from some children who create as a natural form of expression without adult stimulation to others who may need varying degrees of teacher guidance and encouragement.

Such forms of creative expression as art, music, and writing are considered the traditional approaches to creative expression. However, the very essence of creative expression is *movement.* Movement as a form of creativity utilizes the body as the instrument of expression. For the young child the most natural form of creative expression is movement.

Because of their nature, children have an inclination for movement and they use this medium as the basic form of creative expression. Movement is the child's universal language, a most important form of communication and a most meaningful way of learning.

Suggested Teaching Procedures for Creative Rhythms

The following teaching procedures are submitted as suggestive points of departure that may be taken in providing learning experiences for children through creative rhythms.

1. The teacher must recognize that in creative rhythms each child's interpretation may vary. For this reason, the teacher's comments to the child should be characterized by praise and encouragement.
2. Although creative rhythms are essentially individual in nature, the teacher should perhaps introduce this type of rhythm to groups of children. This helps to avoid embarrassment of children and tends to build their confidence.
3. The group may be dispersed informally about the activity area. Formal arrangement is not always conducive to creativity.
4. If there is to be accompaniment, the children listen to it for the purpose of becoming accustomed to its tempo and mood.
5. The children should be given an opportunity to discuss the accompaniment in terms of "what is says" and "how it makes us feel."
6. The children can give their creative interpretation to the accompaniment.
7. Some children may be selected to show their interpretations to the rest of the class. This procedure provides a medium for evaluation.

MOVEMENT SONGS

Movement songs have traditionally been referred to as *singing games.* This designation, however, is changing, at least in the literature, where there seems to be more of a trend to refer to this form of rhythmic play as movement songs. A reason advanced by Dauer and Pangrazi[1] as to why the term singing games is losing favor in present-day terminology is that few of the songs can accurately be called games.

---

1. Dauer, Victor P. and Pangrazi, Robert P., *Dynamic Physical Education for Elementary School Children*, 6th ed. (Minneapolis, Burgess Publishing Company, 1979), pp. 206–207.

Movement songs are actually dances with relatively simple patterns that children perform to their own singing accompaniment or, as in the case of recorded accompaniment, when the singing is furnished by others. Some years ago Kraus[2] suggested the following classification of these kinds of activities:

1. Those which enact simple stories or imitate the actions of everyday life.
2. Those which are based on familiar nursery rhymes or folktales.
3. Those which involve choosing partners.
4. Those in which children follow the leader in improvising rhythmic actions.

Suggested Procedures for Teaching Movement Songs

The following teaching procedures are submitted as suggestive points of departure that may be taken in providing learning experiences for children through movement songs.

1. The teacher and/or the children can sing the entire song.
2. The teacher may wish to have the children discuss the song in terms of what it says.
3. The song can then be sung by phrases, with the teacher singing a phrase and then the children repeating the phrase.
4. The phrases can then be put together with the children singing the whole song.
5. The movement pattern that goes with the song can then be introduced and the song and activity can be combined.
6. In cases where the movement song is long and has several verses, each verse and the activity that goes with the verse can be learned. All verses can then be combined into the whole movement song.
7. Depending upon the movement involved, movement songs can be vigorous activities for children. Because voices tend to tire when activity is engaged in while singing, it may be a wise practice not to have too many movement songs in succession.

---

2. Kraus, Richard. *A Pocket Guide of Folk and Square Dances and Singing Games for the Elementary School* (Englewood Cliffs, NJ, Prentice-Hall), 1966.

DANCES

There are many ways to classify structured dances, and usually these ways are based on the philosophy (also the whims) of the person doing the classifying. Some people like to classify structured dances on the bases of organization; for example, circle dances, longways dances, and the like. Others might classify them according to what is done in the dance; for example, "greeting and meeting" dances. One particular thing that needs to be taken into account, regardless of the way one tends to classify structured dances, is that there will be a certain amount of overlapping in any classification.

Two broad classifications dealt with here are *folk* dances and *square* dances. Folk dances, sometimes referred to as *ethnic* or *nationality* dances, can be described as the dances of a given country which have evolved nationally and spontaneously in conjunction with the everyday activities and experiences of the people who developed them. The dance patterns are performed in group formation and range from simple to rather complex forms. For the most part folk dances used in American schools have been derived from Great Britain and Europe, although some have their origin in our own country.

Square dancing appears to be uniquely American in origin. It is sometimes referred to as American *country* dancing or *Western* dancing. The square dance gets its name from the starting position of the dancers which is that of a quadrille or square.

Suggested Teaching Procedures for Folk and Square Dances

The following teaching procedures are submitted as suggestive points of departure that may be taken in providing learning experiences for children through folk and square dances.

1. The name of the dance should be given. If the teacher knows where the dance got its name (and if this seems important to the learning situation), the teacher can give this information to the children.
2. If the teacher feels that it is important to the learning situation, the background of the dance can be given with respect to the culture of the people who previously danced it, when they danced it, and for what purpose.
3. The introductory discussion of the dance should not be so intense and involved that it detracts from actual participation in the dance.

It should be remembered that the greatest appreciation is likely to come from engaging in the dance.

4. Have the children listen to the accompaniment to become acquainted with the tempo and mood. Give them an opportunity to discuss the accompaniment.

5. Introduce the various movement patterns using appropriate auditory and visual input. Give the children an opportunity to practice the patterns.

6. Teach one part of the dance at a time, adding each part after the preceding part is learned. This procedure will depend to some extent upon the length and complexity of the dance. If it is short, the children may be able to learn the entire dance.

7. All of the parts and accompaniment should be put together into the whole dance.

RHYTHMIC PLAY STORIES

Falling Leaves (creative)

Leaves fall.
They fall from the trees.
They fall to the ground.
Fall like leaves.
Down, down, down.
Down to the ground.
Quiet leaves.
Rest like leaves.
    Could you dance like falling leaves?

The Growing Flowers (creative)

Flowers grow.
First they are seeds.
Be a seed.
Grow like a flower.
Grow and grow.
Keep growing.
Grow tall.
Now you are a flower.
    Could you grow like a flower?

We Dance (dance)

We hold hands.
We make a ring.
We swing our arms.
We swing.
We swing.
We take four steps in.
We take four steps out.
We drop our hands.
We turn about.
Could you do this dance?

Clap and Tap (dance)

I clap with my hands.
Clap, clap, clap.
I tap with my foot.
Tap, tap, tap.
I point my toe.
And around I go.
Clap, clap, clap.
Tap, tap, tap.
Could you do this dance with a friend?

Skip with a Partner (movement song)

Can you sing and dance to "Skip to my Loo"?
Then sing these new words.
Now dance as you sing.

Stand, stand, stand in line.
Stand, stand, stand in line.
Stand, stand, stand in line.
Hold the hand of a partner.
Skip, skip, two by two.
Skip, skip, two by two.
Skip, skip, two by two.
Round and round with your partner.
Skip back, take your seat.
Skip back, take your seat.
Skip back, take your seat.
Skip to your seat, my partner.

Could you skip and sing as you dance with a partner?

Swing Around (movement song)

Do you know the song, "Mary Had a Little Lamb"?
There are other words to this tune.
Sing these words.
They will tell you what to do.
Take your partner's hand.
All sing these words to the same tune as "Mary Had a Little Lamb."
Do what the words say.

Walk with partners round and round.
Walk around, walk around.
Swing your partner round and round.
Swing and swing around.
Skip with partner round and round.
Skip around, skip around.
Swing your partner round and round.
Swing and swing around.

Could you learn these words and then do the dance with a partner?

Around the Ring (movement song)

Do you know a song about hunting?
It is called "A Hunting We Will Go."
Here is one way to do it.
Children hold hands in a ring.
Sing these words.
Sing them like you would sing "A Hunting We Will Go."

Oh! Around the ring we go.
Around the ring we go.
We stop right here.
We clap our hands.
And then sit down just so.

Would you like to do this dance with some other children?

The Parade (creative)

A parade! A parade!
Let's have a parade!
Get a drum or old pan and a stick.
Who will beat the drum?
He will be the leader of the parade.
He will beat the drum, "Boom! Boom! Boom!"
All the children will follow the leader.

Here is the surprise.

When the drum does not say "Boom! Boom! Boom!" sit down at once.

Try not to be the last one to sit down.

"Boom! Boom! Boom!" Will the leader surprise you?

What do you like about this parade?

Swing Your Partner (movement song)

Everyone knows "Farmer in the Dell."

Here is a new way to play it.

Find a partner.

Take your partner's hand.

Do what the words say.

Do it to the tune of "Farmer in the Dell."

We skip around and sing.
We skip around and sing.
We stop ourselves and turn about.
Then with our arms we swing.

We run around and sing.
We run around and sing.
We stop ourselves and turn about.
Then with our arms we swing.

We hop around and sing.
We hop around and sing.
We stop ourselves and turn about.
Then with our arms we swing.

Would you like to find a partner and do this dance?

Find Your Partner (movement song)

Do you like Christmas songs?

I like one called "Jingle Bells."

I know some words you could sing to the tune of "Jingle Bells."

You could play a game as you sing the song.

This is the way to play

Have two circles.

Girls form a circle on the outside.

Boys form a circle on the inside.

Each boy has a girl for a partner.

Remember your partner.

When you start to sing the song, begin to walk.

Boys will walk one way around the circle.

Girls will walk the other way.
At the end of the song, find your partner.
When you do, take hands and both stoop down.
Try not to be the last one down.
This is the song.
Remember to sing it to the tune of "Jingle Bells."

> *Walk around, walk around.*
> *Walk around the ring.*
> *Oh, what fun it is to walk around the ring and sing.*
> *Look around, look around.*
> *Look around the town.*
> *Find your partner when you can and every one stoop down.*

Maybe some children could sing while others play the game?

Could you learn the song to the tune of "Jingle Bells" and play the game with other children?

We Make Up a Dance (dance)

One day Miss Jones asked the children in her class if they would like to make up a dance.
The children were very happy because they liked to dance.
They thought they could start the dance by holding hands and making a circle.
After they made the circle, they all said,

> *Let us slide to the right.*
> *Let us slide, slide, slide.*
> *Let us slide to the left.*
> *Let us slide, slide, slide.*
> *Now let us turn to right all the way around.*
> *Now let us turn to the left and all sit down.*

Could you get some other children to help work out this dance?

The Yankee Doodle Dance (dance)

We all like to sing "Yankee Doodle."
Do you know the tune?
I know a dance we could do.
Here is how we could do it.
We make a circle with first a boy, then a girl.
The girl on the boy's right is his partner.
Try to learn these words to the tune of Yankee Doodle.
Here is the first part.

We circle left, we circle left,
We circle left and mind you.
Now don't forget to swing that girl,
The girl you left behind you.

Here is the second part.

Take your partner by the hand,
And walk with her around, sir.
Now you swing her arm in arm,
And sit right down beside her.

Put both parts together.
Sing as you do the whole dance.
Choose a new partner.
Do the dance again.

We circle left, we circle left,
We circle left and mind you.
Now don't forget to swing that girl,
The girl you left behind you.

Take your partner by the hand,
And walk with her around, sir.
Now you swing her arm in arm,
And sit right down beside her.

Would you like to try to learn this dance with friends?

Swinging and Swaying (movement song)

Can you swing and sway to music?
Here are new words to "Rock-A–Bye, Baby."
As you sing the words, can you think of different ways to swing and sway?

Swinging and swaying go to and fro.
Sway in the breeze, turn round as you go.
Swinging and swaying, go to and fro.

Could you do something different with your hands each time you sway to this song?

A Circle Dance (dance)

Have you heard the tune "Pop Goes the Weasel?"
Find other children who know the tune.
Join hands and make a circle.
Here are some words to sing to the tune of "Pop Goes the Weasel."
Do what the words say.

Now here we go around the ring,
And now we stop together.
And now we walk to the center of the ring,
Just like birds of a feather.

We now step back and stamp one foot,
And all turn round together.
We all join hands and circle again,
In any kind of weather.

Could you show some friends how to do this dance?

Chapter 10

STUNT PLAY READING CONTENT

S tunt play is concerned predominantly with certain kinds of imitations and the performance of a variety of kinds of feats that utilize
such abilities as balance, coordination, flexibility, agility, and strength.
Also included are various kinds of body rolls and springs that encourage
the development of these same abilities.

At the primary level, children should be given the opportunity to
participate in stunt play activities commensurate with their ability. For
example, stunts which involve imitations of animals are of great interest
to boys and girls at this age level. Activities which involve some of the
simple rolls are also suitable.

Stunt play at the intermediate level should be somewhat more advanced,
provided the child has had previous experience and teaching in them at
the primary level. Activities that involve more advanced rolls and various kinds of body springs may be successfully introduced. In a like
manner, more difficult kinds of balance stands may be used in the stunt
play program.

SOME VALUES OF STUNT PLAY ACTIVITIES

One of the major values ordinarily attributed to stunt play activities is
their specific contribution to such elements of physical fitness as strength,
agility, coordination, and flexibility. Zealous proponents of stunt play
activities stoutly maintain that contributions to these various factors are
more likely to accrue through these activities than may be the case
through games and rhythmic activities. The reason for this lies in the
fact that successful performance of certain of the stunt play activities
requires involvement of the various elements of physical fitness.

It has also been suggested by many teachers that some of these kinds of
activities help to build courage, confidence, and poise in children, although
this is difficult to evaluate objectively.

An important value of stunt play activities, but one that is often overlooked, is the contribution that might be made to *tactile perception*. In this regard, it has been suggested that through such activities where the body touches the surface area, the child is given the opportunity to explore the environment *tactilely* with the various body segments.

SUGGESTED TEACHING PROCEDURES
FOR STUNT PLAY ACTIVITIES

The following list suggests some procedures that might be used in teaching stunt play activities.

1. Activities should be selected which correspond with the needs and interests of the group. As mentioned previously, for example, primary level children enjoy stunts that involve imitations of animals. In teaching this type of stunt the teacher should give the children an opportunity to suggest their own ideas of the various animal imitations.
2. Tell the children the name of the activity and ask what it suggests to them.
3. The activity should be described by an explanation of the *whole* activity.
4. Demonstrate or have one or more children demonstrate the entire activity.
5. The demonstrator should then go through the activity position by position, showing the step-by-step procedure involved in its performance.
6. The whole activity should be performed again.
7. The children should be given the opportunity to practice the activity with the teacher and other children observing performance.
8. Select one or more children who perform the activity fairly well and have the other children evaluate the good elements of their performance. ("What did you like about the way Johnny did that stunt?")
9. Have all the children perform the activity again in groups, evaluating their own performance as well as that of others.

STUNT PLAY STORIES

The Funny Clown

I am a funny clown.
I move like a funny clown.
I Jump.
I skip.
I run.
I stop.
I have fun.
   Could you move around like a funny clown?

Circus Elephant

I saw the circus.
I saw many animals.
I saw an elephant.
He was big.
He had big legs.
He took big steps.
He had a trunk.
He swings his trunk.
I will walk like the elephant.
   Could you walk so that you would look like the elephant swinging
his trunk?

Curly Cat Takes a Walk

Curly Cat is asleep.
Curly Cat opens his eyes.
Curly Cat takes a walk.
He walks with long steps.
He holds his head high.
He walks all around.
Try to walk like Curly Cat.
Put your hands on the floor.
Walk all around like Curly Cat.
   Could you walk so you would look like Curly Cat?

Grizzly Bear

I saw a Grizzly Bear.
Grizzly Bear was at the zoo.
He walked and walked.
I can walk like Grizzly Bear.

I can put my hands on the floor.
I walk on my hands and feet.
I walk and walk.
I say, "Gr-Gr-Gr."
    Could you walk so you would look like Grizzly Bear?

George Giraffe

There is a tall animal in a faraway land.
He has a long neck.
His name is George Giraffe.
You could look like him if you did this.
Place your arms high over your head.
Put your hands together.
Point them to the front.
This will be his neck and head.
Now walk like George Giraffe.
This is how.
Stand on your toes.
Walk with your legs straight.
    Could you walk so you would look like George Giraffe?

The Jumping Rabbit

I can jump like a rabbit.
I sit like a rabbit.
I hold my hands on the floor.
Now I jump.
My feet come up to my hands.
I hold my hands way out.
I put my hands on the floor.
I jump again.
I jump again and again.
    How many rabbit jumps can you take?

Kangaroo at the Zoo

Take a trip to the zoo.
You will see a kangaroo.
He hops far.
Can you?
Hop like the kangaroo.
Take one hop.
Take two.
Do like the kangaroo.

Could you do like the kangaroo?

The Spider

Have you ever watched the way spiders walk?
They have long legs.
They put them way out.
Try to walk like a spider.
Put your hands on the floor.
Keep your arms straight.
Keep your legs straight.
Walk to the front.
Walk to one side.
Walk to the other side.
Walk to the back.
Walk all around like a spider.
   Would you like to try to walk like a spider?

Chester Crow

Chester Crow is a big black bird.
He can hop.
You can hop like Chester.
Bend your knees.
Put your arms out.
Your arms are wings.
Hop like Chester Crow.
   How many crow hops can you take?

The Lame Puppy

I saw a lame puppy.
The lame puppy walked.
He held up one leg.
He walked on three legs.
I walk like this puppy.
I hold up one leg.
I walk around.
   Could you walk like a lame puppy?

The Bouncing Bear

Once there was a bear.
His name was Bouncing Bear.
He bounced by jumping.

He jumped up and down on his toes.
He bounced here.
He bounced there.
He bounced and bounced.
　　Could you bounce like Bouncing Bear?

Casper Camel

Casper Camel lives in the zoo.
He has a hump on his back
Could you look like Casper Camel?
You will need a hump.
Try it this way.
Bend forward.
Put your hands behind your back.
Hold them together.
That will be a hump.
That will look like Casper
Could you move like Casper Camel?
Take a step.
Lift your head.
Take a step.
Lift your head.
Move like Casper Camel.
　　Do you think it would be fun to walk like Casper Camel?

Sidney Seal

Did you ever hear of a sea lion?
Sometimes he is called a seal.
He lives in the sea.
Sometimes he lives in the zoo.
There is one in the zoo called Sidney Seal.
He likes to swim.
He can also walk on land.
Would you like to try to walk like Sidney Seal?
Try it this way.
Put your hands on the floor.
Put your feet back.
Put your weight on your hands and on top of your toes.
Now walk on your hands and drag your legs.
This is the way to walk like Sidney Seal.
　　Do you think you could walk like Sidney Seal?

Rocking Chair

There are many kinds of chairs.
One kind of chair is a rocking chair.
It rocks and rocks.
Two children can become a rocking chair.
They sit facing each other.
They sit on each other's feet.
They rock and rock.
Could you play rocking chair with another child?

The Clowns Do a Stunt

Have you ever seen clowns at a circus?
Sometimes they do funny things.
Once I saw two clowns do a stunt together.
This is what they did.
They sat back to back.
Their feet were flat on the floor.
Their feet were close to their bodies.
They locked their arms together.
They pushed hard.
As they pushed they began to rise.
At last they were standing.
They sat down and did the stunt again.
Could you do this stunt with a friend?

The Little King

In a faraway country across the sea lives a Little King.
This Little King stands straight and tall.
He folds his arms in front of him.
He crosses one foot over the other.
He sits down slowly.
Now the Little King wants to get up.
He keeps his arms the same way.
He keeps his feet the same way.
He rises in this way.
Now he stands straight again.
Could you sit and stand like Little King?

Thread the Needle

Have you ever seen your mother sew?
First she threads the needle.
There is a stunt called "Thread the Needle."
Can you think of how you would do it?
This is how.
Clasp your hands in front of you.
This is the needle's eye.
Bend forward.
Step through the clasped hands with one foot.
Follow with the other foot.
Bring the first foot back.
Bring the other foot back.
That is how you thread the needle.
Try it.
Could you show a friend how to thread the needle?

Oliver Ostrich

There is a big bird at the zoo.
His name is Oliver Ostrich.
How could you look like Oliver Ostrich?
I wonder if you could walk like Oliver Ostrich?
Shall we try?
First, bend forward.
Keep your knees straight.
Hold your ankles.
Now walk.
Walk like Oliver Ostrich.
How do you think it would feel to walk like Oliver Ostrich?

A Stunt for Two

Did you ever wring out a cloth?
You turn it very tightly and the water comes out.
Did you know there is a stunt called "Wring the Dishcloth?"
Two people are needed to do this stunt.
Find a friend to do this stunt with you.
Face your friend.
Hold hands.
Raise your arms to one side.
Turn with your friend under the raised arms.
Now you are back to back with your friend.

Raise the arms to the other side.
Both friends turn.
You will pass under the raised arms.
Try it again and again.
   How many times can you wring the dishcloth with your friend?

A Strange Way to Walk

Did you know that there are many ways to walk?
You can walk forward.
You can walk backward.
You can walk sideward.
Then you can walk on your hands and feet at the same time.
I know a strange way to walk on your hands and feet.
This is the way you do it.
First, you sit down and place your hands behind you.
Now you raise your body.
You will be facing upward.
From this position try to walk on your hands and feet.
Walk forward, walk backward, and walk sideward.
   How far can you walk in this position?

A Topsy-Turvey Stunt

Do you know what "topsy-turvy" means?
It is one way of saying "upside down."
You can do a topsy-turvy stunt.
This is how.
Squat down.
Put your hands beside you on the floor.
Point your fingers toward your feet.
Make your legs straight.
Now you are on your hands and heels.
Walk backward on your hands pulling your heels.
   Could you show a friend how to do this topsy-turvy stunt?

The Jumping Stunt

Do you like to jump?
Most children do.
Did you know that there are many ways to jump?
There are some easy ways to jump.
There are also some difficult ways to jump.
Let me tell you about one difficult way to jump.

This is the way to do it.
First, stand straight with the feet close together.
Next, bend your knees.
Bend low enough so you can grasp your ankles with your hands.
Now try to jump.
Jump a short distance first.
Then jump a longer distance.
See how many ankle jumps you can take.
See how far you can jump this way.
  Could you show some of your friends how to jump this way?

Going Up! Going Down!

"Going up! Going down! is a new stunt.
It is about an elevator.
An elevator goes up.
It ascends.
An elevator goes down.
It descends.
You can play you are an elevator.
This is the way.
Squat way down.
Slowly straighten up as you say, "Going up."
Slowly squat again as you say, "Going down."
Isn't it fun to be an elevator?
  Could you be an elevator and go up and down?

Mr. Centipede

Do you know the name of a little animal that has many legs?
It is called a centipede.
You and some other boys could join together and look like a centipede.
This is the way to do it.
The boys stand behind one another.
Now they are standing in a row.
The boys put their feet apart.
All boys bend forward.
All boys put their right hands between their knees.
The boy behind reaches forward with his left hand.
He grasps the right hand of the boy in front of him.
Now the boys are all joined.
They look like a centipede.
  Could you find some friends and walk like a centipede?

We would like to conclude by stating again that all of the practices presented in this book have been carefully researched and extensively field tested with large numbers of children. They have been found to meet with great success when applied in the appropriate manner.

BIBLIOGRAPHY

Almy, M. A child's right to play. *Young Children,* May 1984.

Anderson, R. C. et al. Do errors on classroom reading tasks slow growth in reading? *Elementary School Journal,* January 1988.

Bagby, M. Play is basic to teaching. *Lutheran Education,* November/December 1985.

Bishop, J. K. Play: Its meaning and being. *Early Child Development and Care,* July 1986.

Boals, B. M. In defense of play. *Contemporary Education,* Summer 1987.

Bruner, J. Play, thought and language. *Peabody Journal of Education,* Spring 1983.

Cadenhead, K. Reading level: A metaphor that shapes practice. *Phi Delta Kappan,* February 1987.

Casbergue, R. M. and Greene, J. F. Persistent misconceptions about sensory perception and reading disability. *Journal of Reading,* December 1988.

Chall, J. S. Reading and early childhood education: The critical issues. *Principal,* May 1987.

Chanoff, D. When play is learning: A school designed for self-directed education. *Phi Delta Kappan,* May 1984.

Collier, R. G. Reading, thinking and play: A child's search for meaning. *Yearbook* (Claremont Reading Conference) 1983.

Ditchburn, S. J. Understanding children's play: A conversational analysis of one instructional strategy. *International Journal of Early Childhood,* October 1986.

Dobbert, M. L. Play is not monkey business: A holistic biocultural perspective on the role of play in learning. *Educational Horizons,* Summer 1985.

Fuchs, L. S. The validity of informal reading comprehension measures. *Remedial and Special Education,* March/April 1988.

Galda. Playing about a story: Its impact on comprehension. *The Reading Teacher,* October 1982.

Gee, T. C. and Forester, N. Moving reading instruction beyond the reading classroom. *Journal of Reading,* March 1988.

Gehlbach, R. D. Children's play and self-education. *Curriculum Inquiry,* Summer 1988.

Gentile, L. M. and Hoot, J. L. Kindergarten play: The foundation of reading. *The Reading Teacher,* January 1983.

Giordano, G. Play learning. *Day Care and Early Education,* Spring 1988.

Grabe, M. et al. Eye fixation patterns during informed and uninformed comprehension monitoring. *Journal of Reading Behaviors,* February 1987.

Greenberg, P. Ideas that work with young children; Learning self-esteem and self-discipline through play. *Young Children,* January 1989.

Grubaugh, S. and Virgilio, S. J., Strategies for the development of reading skills through physical education. *Reading Improvement,* Summer 1985.

Hagedorn, J. All work and no play. *The Times Educational Supplement,* May 30, 1986.

Henk, W. A., Reading assessments of the future. *The Reading Teacher,* May 1987.

Hillerich, R. L. The problems with readability formulas. *Early Years,* January 1987.

Hopkins, D. The serious purpose behind child's play. *The Times Educational Supplement,* December 12, 1987.

Honig, A. S. Playtime learning games for young children. *Day Care and Early Education,* Fall 1982.

Humphrey, J. H. How children can learn about reading through dance activities, Chapter 9 in *Child Development and Learning Through Dance.* New York, AMS Press, Inc., 1987.

Humphrey, J. H. *Teaching Gifted Children Through Motor Learning.* Springfield, Illinois, Charles C Thomas Publisher, 1985.

Humphrey, J. H. and Humphrey, J. N. *Help Your Child Learn the 3Rs Through Active Play.* Springfield, Illinois, Charles C Thomas . Publisher, 1980.

Isenberg, J. and Quisenberg, N. L. Play: A necessity for all children. *Childhood Education,* February 1988.

John, E. L. Unlocking the mystery of the nonreading child. *English Journal,* November 1988.

Koenke, K. Readability formulas: Use and misuse. *The Reading Teacher,* March 1987.

Learning through play, *Forecast of the Home Economist,* November/December 1987.

Mehran, M., and White, K. R. Parent tutoring as a supplement to compensatory education for first grade children. *Remedial and Special Education,* May/June 1988.

Pany, D., and McCoy, K. M., Effects of corrective feedback on word accuracy and reading comprehension of readers with learning disabilities. *Journal of Learning Disabilities,* November 1988.

Parrish, B. Reading practices and possibilities in physical education. *Journal of Physical Education, Recreation and Dance,* March 1984.

Parrish, B. Sporting proposition: Reading in the physical education curriculum. *Reading World,* October 1982.

Pellegrini, A. D. Rough-and-tumble play: Developmental and educational significance. *Educational Psychologist,* Winter 1987.

Pelligrini, A. D. et al. Saying what you mean: Using play to teach literate language. *Language Arts,* March 1983.

Pinsent, P. The implications of recent research into early reading. *Early Child Development and Care,* September 1988.

Play in education, Prospects, July 1986.

Rush, R. T. Assessing readability: Formulas and alternatives. *The Reading Teacher,* December 1985.

Sadoski, M. et al. Imagination in story responses: Relationship between imagery, affect, and structured importance. *Reading Research Quarterly,* Spring 1988.

Saracho, O. N. Cognitive style characteristics as related to young children's play behaviors. *Early Child Development and Care,* April 1987.

Saracho, O. N. Young children's play behaviors and cognitive styles. *Early Child Development and Care,* July 1985.

Sarland, C., Piaget, Blyton, and story: Children's play and the reading process. *Children's Literature in Education,* Summer 1985.

Schubert, D. G., and Walton, H. N. Eye movements—more than meets the eye. *The New England Reading Association Journal,* Spring 1987.

Tovey, D. R. et al. Beginning reading: A natural language learning process. *Childhood Education,* June 1988.

Terrell, B. Y. and Schwartz, R. G. Object transformations in the play of language-impaired children. *Journal of Speech and Hearing Disorders,* November 1988.

Wardle, F. Getting back to basics of children's play. *Child Care Information Exchange,* September 1987.

Westlake, G. When child's play is serious business. *Forecast for Home Economics,* September 1984.

Wolfgang, C. H., and Sanders, T. S. Defending young children's play as the ladder to literacy. *Theory Into Practice,* Spring 1981.

van der Kooii, R. and Meyes, H. P. Research on children's play. *Prospects,* September 1986.

INDEX

163